595.78942337 WAC

3

LEARNING
services

01209 722146

Duchy College Rosewarne
Learning Centre

This resource is to be returned on or before the last date
stamped below. To renew items please contact the Centre

Three Week Loan

A
Cornwall
Butterfly
Atlas

BY JOHN WACHER, JOHN WORTH AND ADRIAN SPALDING

with contributions from
Steve Bassett, Paul Browning, Phil Harris, Stephen Hoskin,
Roger Lane and Lee Slaughter

Published by Pisces Publications
in conjuction with
Cornwall Butterfly Conservation

First published 2003 by Pisces Publications in conjuction with Cornwall Butterfly Conservation. Pisces Publications is the imprint of **Nature**Bureau (formerly the Nature Conservation Bureau Limited).

British Library-in-Publication Data
A catalogue record for this book is available from the British Library.

ISBN 1-874357-23-4

Designed and produced by **Nature**Bureau, 36 Kingfisher Court, Hambridge Road, Newbury, Berkshire RG14 5SJ.

Printed by Information Press, Oxford.

CONTENTS

ACKNOWLEDGEMENTS
AND PHOTOGRAPHIC CREDITS

The authors would like to thank all those listed below who have allowed their photographs to be used for this book:
Adam Sharpe for preparing the drawings in Chapter 1; Sarah Wacher who prepared the first typewritten draft of the text and
Barbara Kane who typed it onto disc. Thanks are also due to all those who lent their photographs for the illustrations.

Title page: A typical coastal habitat with Silver-studded Blues, from a painting by Barry Olfield.

Page 3: The geology of Cornwall. Adam Sharpe (*after R.M. Barton*)

Page 4: Dune formation at Upton Towans. To the left of centre can be seen one of the surviving bunkers of the Nobel Explosive Works. John Wacher

Page 5: A bridleway flanked by Cornish hedges near Hayle. John Wacher

Page 6: Coastal Heathland between Gwennap Head and Carn Guthensbrâs. John Wacher

Page 7: Average daily hours of sunshine in July from 1961–90. Adam Sharpe (*after the Meteorological Office*)

Page 7: Mean annual rainfall. Adam Sharpe (*after the Meteorological Office*)

Page 8: Mean maximum and minimum day temperatures in January from 1961–90. Adam Sharpe (*after the Meteorological Office*)

Page 8: Mean maximum and minimum day temperatures in July from 1961–90 Adam Sharpe (*after the Meteorological Office*)

Page 9: A typical fritillary site at Bunny's Hill. Lee Slaughter

Page 16: Small Skipper. Steve Bassett

Page 18: Essex Skipper. Lee Slaughter

Page 20: Lulworth Skipper. Lee Slaughter

Page 21: Large Skipper. Lee Slaughter

Page 23: Dingy Skipper. Steve Bassett

Page 25: Grizzled Skipper. Lee Slaughter

Page 26: Grizzled Skipper, ab. *taras*. Paul Browning

Page 27: Wood White. Graham Sutton

Page 29: Pale Clouded Yellow. Kars Veling

Page 31: Berger's Clouded Yellow. Paul Browning

Page 33: Clouded Yellow. Paul Browning

Page 33: Clouded Yellow, f. *helice*. Lee Slaughter

Page 34: Brimstone. Sally Foster

Page 36: Large White. Steve Bassett

Page 38: Small White. Steve Bassett

Page 40: Green-veined White. Steve Bassett

Page 42: Bath White. Paul Browning

Page 44: Male Orange-tip. Paul Browning

Page 45: Female Orange-tip. Lee Slaughter

Page 46: Green Hairstreak. Adrian Spalding

Page 48: Brown Hairstreak. Paul Browning

Page 49: Purple Hairstreak. Paul Browning

Page 52: White-letter Hairstreak. Steve Bassett

Page 54: Small Copper. Lee Slaughter

Page 55: Small Copper, ab. *caeruleopunctata*. Sally Foster

Page 55: Small Copper, ab. *schmidtii*. Charlie David

Page 56: Long-tailed Blue, captured at Pentewan in 2001. Lee Slaughter

Page 57: Small Blue. Lee Slaughter

Page 59: Short-tailed Blue. Paul Browning

Page 60: Silver-studded Blue. Steve Bassett

Page 62: Silver-studded Blue, ab. Paul Browning

Page 63: Brown Argus. Paul Browning

Page 65: Common Blue, blue female. Adrian Spalding

Page 67: Holly Blue. Paul Browning

Page 69: Cornish Large Blue, pre-extinction. Tom Jenkins

Page 70: Sometime Large Blue habitat at Tidna. Adrian Spalding

Page 70: Release of re-introduced Large Blues in 2000. Adrian Spalding

Page 70: Large Blue, Cornish re-introduction. Lee Slaughter

Page 71: White Admiral. Steve Bassett

Page 73: Red Admiral. Lee Slaughter

Page 75: Painted Lady. Lee Slaughter

Page 75: Painted Lady, ab. *pallida*. Steven Jones

Page 77: Small Tortoiseshell. Mary Tout

Page 79: Large Tortoiseshell. Paul Browning

Page 81: Camberwell Beauty. Adrian Spalding

Page 83: Peacock. Leon Truscott

Page 85: Comma, ab. *hutchinsoni*. Paul Browning

Page 87: Small Pearl-bordered Fritillary. Steve Bassett

Page 88: Small Pearl-bordered Fritillary, underside. Lee Slaughter

Page 88: Pearl-bordered Fritillary, underside. Lee Slaughter

LIST OF TABLES

LIST OF SPONSORS

Since this book is a co-operative work by the Cornwall Branch of Butterfly Conservation, the Committee would like to thank all those, especially other branches, who contributed to the cost of production; in all about £4,000 was raised. Without this sum, and their sponsorship, there would have been no book.

The Committee's special thanks must go to the Chairman, Lee Slaughter, who was largely responsible for organising the Appeal and who was personally responsible for raising much of the sponsorship.

BUTTERFLY CONSERVATION BRANCHES

Bedfordshire & Northamptonshire Branch
Cambridge & Essex Branch
Devon Branch
East Scotland Branch
Hertfordshire and Middlesex Branch
Kent Branch
Lancashire Branch (Tom Wallace)
Lincolnshire Branch
Surrey Branch
West Midlands Branch

COMPANIES AND OTHER ORGANISATIONS

Anon
Beech Motors (St Austell) Ltd
Bennett, Jones & Co
Bryan Eddy Financial Planning
Crowe Insurance Group
Derek Slaughter (Insurance Services) Ltd
English Nature
Gwithian Green Residents Association
Lloyds TSB Bank (St Austell Branch)
Norwich Union Insurance (Plymouth)
South West Optics
Spalding Associates (Environmental) Ltd
The National Trust

INDIVIDUALS

Mr J.P. & A.F. Barker; Mr T.G. Barr; Natasha & Alexandra Bassett; Mr R. Bedford; Mr A. & Mrs P. Berriman; Miss Lisa Best, (Mrs Lisa Slaughter); Mr Phil H. Boggis; Mr D. Bridges; Mr Paul R.G. Browning; Mr D. Cheesman; Miss F. Coley; Mr John B. Cooke; Mr P.S. Drayson; Dr Clifford Edwards; M.T. Farmer; Mrs Lynn Fomison; Mr J.M. & Mrs S.M. Foster; Dr Paul Gainey; Mr Phil Harris; J. Herbert; Mr A.J. Higginson; Miss Carly Hoskin; Mrs Claire Hoskin; Mr G.J. Kingerlee; Mr Roger Lane; Mr Chris Larkby; Ms C.A. & Mr M. Lee; Mr A.G. & E.E. Mackonochie; Mr P.R. Main; Mrs J.B. Mallett; Mr S. Marples; Mr G. & N.M. Martin; Mr B.W. Ofield; Dr T.G. Osmond; Mr J.M. Randall; L.M.P. Schofield; Mr B.T. & Mrs M.C. Shaw; Mr Lee Slaughter; James & Jessica Slaughter; Mr Derek H.V. Slaughter; Mr J. Smith; Mr Adrian Spalding; Dr B.R. & A.A. Stevens; Mr P.L. & A.P. Stiles; Dr J. Summerscales; Mr G. Sutton; Mr H.A. Tout; Mrs M.C. Tout; Mr L.A.C. Truscott; Mr M. Tunmore; Mr C.M. Tyler-Smith; Prof. J.S. Wacher; Mr K.R. & Mrs R.G. Wasley; Mrs P. Williams; Mr D. Worton.

AUTHORS' NOTE
EXPLANATION OF MAPS

This book is not intended to be an identification manual, nor does it contain life histories of Cornish butterflies. Readers who require this information are directed to the many existing books on British species.

The book's primary aims are that it should be both readable and informative about the county's butterflies. It includes accounts of all species that have been, or are now, resident in Cornwall, together with sections on the several migrants which have occurred in the county, arranged in taxonomic order. The species accounts include specifically Cornish information, where this is available, and show larval foodplants, distribution and flight periods in the county; the latter are often different from the rest of Britain, with butterflies appearing both earlier and later than elsewhere. The distribution maps, though, suffer one failing, common to all such maps, that they often show the density of recorders and not that of the butterflies, especially with the more abundant species. For instance the 10 km squares (SW 62) which includes Kynance Cove has recently been poorly recorded, although it is probably the most visited part of the Lizard peninsula. Yet in 1994 three recorders found the Large Skipper there on four separate occasions. No doubt this butterfly is still flying there, but does not figure in the 1995–2000 record. Most records from visitors tend to be from the coastal footpath, while recorders resident in Cornwall tend to concentrate on the coast and some well-known inland sites. Moreover, access is probably easier on the coast, while attempts to follow inland routes often result in finding footpaths blocked with brambles and nettles, usually from neglect, and occasionally barbed wire. It is also difficult to assess from the maps whether a species has genuinely declined or increased in the last decade or so, since, unfortunately, the pre-1995 distribution (yellow dots) may be partly obscured by the post-1994 distribution (green dots). So the maps only show changes in the distributions between the two periods, or possibly of recorders for the commonest butterflies. Flight period diagrams are only included for those species for which there are sufficient Cornish records, and represent the situation only between 1995–2001. Moreover, for some very rare or migrant species, the sections on conservation and aberration have been omitted.

The regional rate of change is based on a comparison of the distribution maps in Heath, Pollard and Thomas (1984) with those in Asher *et al.* (2001), and show changes in Cornwall, Devon and Somerset; in some cases these apparent changes may be due to increased recording.

The nomenclature followed is that of the *Millennium Atlas* (Asher *et al.* 2001) and where the genus has recently been altered the former name has been given in brackets. The names of larval foodplants follow those adopted by the *Flora of Cornwall* (French *et al.* 1999).

Most of the illustrations of butterflies and of the aberrations are photographs of live Cornish specimens taken by branch members in Cornish habitats, except for some, where rarity precluded it; needless to say, all habitat illustrations are in Cornwall, and show the wide-ranging types of locality contained within the county in which butterflies breed.

PREFACE

Jeremy Thomas
Vice-president, Butterfly Conservation

I warmly welcome the publication of this excellent atlas of Cornish butterflies. Not only does it represent ten years of rigorous, co-ordinated recording by butterfly enthusiasts throughout the County, but it also contains a scholarly collation of earlier records, together with the authors' interpretations of their maps and authoritative accounts of the changes in status and local requirements of every butterfly species described. At a national level, this greatly enhances the series of atlases that have been published for several other Counties in recent years: from a Cornish perspective, this first atlas of butterfly distributions perfectly complements three other fine books on Lepidoptera that were published in the last decade.

Cornwall possesses an exciting range of butterfly species compared to most other UK counties, reflecting its warm climate, its varied terrain and the many habitats favoured by scarce or local species. Although not exempt from some of the losses that have afflicted less favoured counties – the account of the once abundant Pearl-bordered Fritillary, for example, makes sombre reading – Cornwall's relatively unspoilt landscapes still support an abundance of species that are scarce or local elsewhere. Mapping and understanding the habitat requirements of the surviving populations of declining species is an essential prerequisite to their conservation, and this book makes an important contribution to this task. Equally valuable will be the enormous pleasure and information that it will provide both to resident naturalists and to the many visitors to Cornwall. For experts and newcomers alike, I am confident that this will be an essential handbook for many years to come.

The authors and many recorders of the Cornish atlas are particularly to be congratulated on the thoroughness with which they have sought out past records and searched for new sites. Nevertheless, it is axiomatic that all atlases of butterflies are to some extent incomplete and, in time, become outdated as species distributions and statuses change. It is my belief that this inspiring book will provide a stimulus, as well as a reference point, for future butterfly recorders in Cornwall. If so, the Cornwall branch of *Butterfly Conservation* will have fulfilled another valuable service to their County.

CHAPTER I

INTRODUCTION

Lee Slaughter
Chairman, Cornwall Butterfly Conservation

I was just seven years old when my father gave me some Brooke Bond Tea card albums, complete with tea cards. They included British Butterflies and Butterflies of the World, both by Richard Ward, and were issued in 1963–64. My father informed me that he had once collected butterflies during his National Service in the 1950s and had kept them in the loft in cardboard boxes. He showed them to me, and they included Comma, Green Hairstreak and Grayling. One warm summer's day shortly afterwards he taught me how to catch butterflies in a makeshift net. I caught a male Small White and spread out its wings with pennies, and a few weeks later it took pride of place on a thin bed of cotton wool in a slim cigar box. I was captivated and my lifelong interest in these beautiful creatures had begun.

Several years later our family moved to Cornwall and the glorious summer of 1976 introduced me to butterflies not seen in a suburban London garden. Silver-washed, High Brown, Dark Green and Small Pearl-bordered Fritillaries, Green Hairstreaks, Brimstones, Gatekeepers, Ringlets and several other species abounded in the Cornish countryside. I decided to try to find all the Cornish species to photograph, but despite all my efforts, I could not locate any book or guide on butterflies in Cornwall. This was partly rectified later by the publication by Frost and Madge of *The Butterflies of South-east Cornwall* in 1991. Then followed in quick succession *Cornwall's Butterfly and Moth Heritage* by Adrian Spalding in 1992, *The Butterflies of Cornwall and the Isles of Scilly* by Roger Penhallurick in 1996 and Frank Smith's magisterial survey, *The Moths and Butterflies of Cornwall and the Isles of Scilly* in 1997.

In the meantime, a meeting of enthusiasts took place in December 1992, which resulted in the formation of the Cornwall branch of Butterfly Conservation, under the chairmanship of Gary Pilkington, which was launched the following June. An ultimate aim of the branch was to publish an atlas of Cornwall's butterflies, but, as an interim measure, Adrian Spalding and John Worth produced for us an annual report, showing distribution maps for each species; in addition we also produced a triannual newsletter, *The Butterfly Observer*. The maps often looked quite sparse, even for the commoner species, equating more with the distribution of recorders. Big steps were taken in the 1990s to co-ordinate and increase the records of our resident and migrant butterflies and many areas of Cornwall have now been well-covered for each.

The branch Committee agreed at its last meeting in the twentieth century that we should proceed with the production of a full-colour atlas, describing each resident, migrant and vagrant species in Cornwall in recent history. The Committee further decided that the necessary funds should be raised by sponsorship, with a minimum of £30, which would entitle the sponsor to a free copy; their name would also be included on a sponsorship page. Our branch was delighted by the generosity of some members, local businesses and several other regional branches of Butterfly Conservation for their response; altogether nearly £4,000 was collected. Grateful thanks must go to our Treasurer, Steve Bassett, for coping with this great increase in funds.

All Committee members have contributed their knowledge to the book as well as sponsorship: Steve Bassett, Paul Browning, Phil Harris, Steve Hoskin, Roger Lane, Adrian Spalding, John Wacher and John Worth; I was also pleased to be able to participate in these accounts. In addition, John Wacher spent several months ensuring that a measure of conformity was pursued throughout the book, as well as compiling the bibliography and gazetteer, while John Worth dedicated many, many hours to collating, sorting and entering the thousands of records, and to producing the final distribution maps and flight period diagrams. Thanks should also go to the branch members and others who have provided the more recent records; it could be claimed that it is their Atlas more than anyone's.

I hope this Atlas will appeal to a wide range of people, and that it will take its place alongside the long sequence of excellent books on Cornish butterflies already published. No matter whether they are a casual visitor to the county, or a holidaymaker who visits annually, but who has an interest in its flora and fauna; the growing band of conservation-minded wildlife lovers; the serious butterfly enthusiast, indeed anyone who is interested in finding out more about the distribution of the county's butterflies. Let us not be complacent though; the publication of this Atlas is not the end of recording but merely a photograph in time of butterfly status at the beginning of the twenty-first century. Time does not stand still and the future of many of our species is not entirely clear. Only by continual recording can we view the constant change in each species' distribution and decide what measures can be taken to conserve these most precious indicators of our wildlife. It is certainly my wish that any future atlas will show an increase in the range of many species rather than a decrease that most other areas of Britain have had to endure. I hope that the increasing demands of modern day life, intensive farming, mismanagement of the countryside, urban sprawl and possible global warming do not have the detrimental effects that are naturally assumed. This publication is designed as a benchmark, from which the more conservation-minded must do whatever possible to ensure that future generations will still enjoy seeing living butterflies in the Cornish countryside and not have to resort to books to tell them where they could once be found. The countryside with fewer butterflies would be a sadder place.

CHAPTER 2

THE CORNISH ENVIRONMENT

All butterflies are sensitive to the environment, which is ever-changing, unless the processes are interrupted by human agency. Consequently, a thorough knowledge of both the natural and man-made environments is necessary if the distribution of butterflies is to be understood.

GEOLOGY

The environment is made up of many factors, of which geology is of fundamental importance, since surface soils are formed from the underlying rocks; it may therefore be said to be the bones of the landscape.

The basic geology of Britain follows a line running very roughly north-east to south-west, with the older rocks of the south-west peninsula, Wales, the Pennines, Lake District and Scotland to the north-west, and the younger oolites and chalks to the south-east. Consequently, as a general rule, but one with many local exceptions, the soils derived from this geology in the former region, of which Cornwall is a part, are mainly acidic.

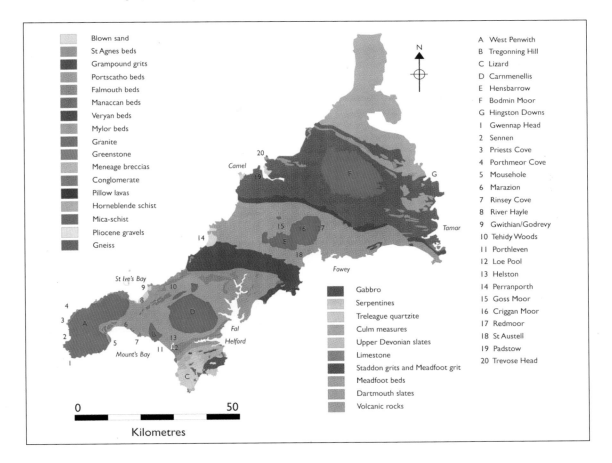

Blown sand	A West Penwith
St Agnes beds	B Tregonning Hill
Grampound grits	C Lizard
Portscatho beds	D Carnmenellis
Falmouth beds	E Hensbarrow
Manaccan beds	F Bodmin Moor
Veryan beds	G Hingston Downs
Mylor beds	1 Gwennap Head
Granite	2 Sennen
Greenstone	3 Priests Cove
Meneage breccias	4 Porthmeor Cove
Conglomerate	5 Mousehole
Pillow lavas	6 Marazion
Horneblende schist	7 Rinsey Cove
Mica-schist	8 River Hayle
Pliocene gravels	9 Gwithian/Godrevy
Gneiss	10 Tehidy Woods
	11 Porthleven
Gabbro	12 Loe Pool
Serpentines	13 Helston
Treleague quartzite	14 Perranporth
Culm measures	15 Goss Moor
Upper Devonian slates	16 Criggan Moor
Limestone	17 Redmoor
Staddon grits and Meadfoot grit	18 St Austell
Meadfoot beds	19 Padstow
Dartmouth slates	20 Trevose Head
Volcanic rocks	

0   50
Kilometres

The geology of Cornwall is complex, and in some respects unique in Britain (Barton 1964). The ground rock of much of the lower-lying parts of the county is, to a great extent, made up of a contorted, sedimentary, slatey material: the killas of the Cornish miner. These rocks, in themselves, are geologically diverse, although broadly belonging to the Devonian series, but in the north-east of the county they are replaced by the carboniferous rocks of the Culm Measures.

The almost uniformly flat plateau of the Lizard, on the other hand, represents an ancient erosion surface, produced in the Pliocene age, when much of west Cornwall was still submerged beneath the sea; it can be broadly divided between a northern area of sedimentary Palaeozoic rocks, and a much larger southern part containing a complex of highly crystalline, metamorphic strata of uncertain age, among which are the serpentines, hornblende-schists and gneisses.

Beneath the whole of the south-west peninsula, from Dartmoor to the Isles of Scilly, lies an intrusive granite ridge of uneven height. Originally it was covered by the overlying killas, but, through a process of denudation, when much of Cornwall lay beneath the sea, the higher domes became exposed, eventually forming the high moors of Cornwall: Bodmin, Hensbarrow, Carnmenellis and Land's End, with smaller exposures at Hingston Down and Tregonning Hill. Surrounding each of these intrusions is a reddened metamorphic aureole, which is heavily mineralised and the source of most Cornish metal ores. The granite/killas interface can be clearly seen in the exposed cliff faces at Porthmeor Cove near Pendeen, at Rinsey Head, at Priest's Cove just south of Cape Cornwall, and at Mousehole.

The granite of Hensbarrow, near St Austell, has been heavily kaolinised, a low-temperature process, in which the feldspars in the granite were attacked by magmatic water and carbon dioxide to produce clay. The commercial exploitation of this valuable mineral has resulted in the wholesale disfigurement of the landscape north of St Austell, with its deep quarries and conical waste heaps of fine white silica sand. To a lesser extent, china clay has also been quarried on Bodmin Moor, and in the Land's End area.

There is little evidence in Cornwall for the Mesozoic or Tertiary geological eras, although it was during the Miocene period of the latter that the county ultimately began to emerge from the sea in a series of intermittent stages, causing a sequence of ancient erosion surfaces to be formed, which now rise like broad steps between the coast and the higher land of the interior. The youngest of these surfaces is considered to belong to the subsequent Pliocene period, during which the Lizard was also formed. Beds of sands, gravels, pebbles and clays were laid down in numerous places in this, and in the following Pleistocene period, when Cornwall was subject to the peri-glacial conditions of the Ice Ages. Evidence for this, and for some of the earlier episodes can also be seen in the raised beaches which occur near Helston, at Porthleven, around Mount's Bay, and in many other places along the coast.

The end of the Ice Ages brought violent flooding and swollen rivers, which swept out all the finer alluvium, leaving only the coarser gravels. But as the climate moderated, flow in the rivers was reduced and the finer sediments were once more deposited, sometimes blocking water-courses, so that the marshes and bogs of the high moors were created, which are now often supplemented by thick beds of peat. Vegetation gradually replaced the tundra of the glacial periods; trees and ferns emerged, but there were still

minor relative movements between land and sea, so that sometimes low-lying forests were submerged, and remains of an ancient forest can often be seen on the beach near Porthleven, and at Mount's Bay, after a storm has removed surface sand.

Most of the rocks and deposits referred to above, apart from the carboniferous limestone, give rise to acid or near-neutral soils. There is, however, one major exception. Particularly on the north coast, but also

Dune formation at Upton Towans. To the left of centre can be seen one of the surviving bunkers of the Nobel Explosive Works.

at one or two places on the south, large tracts of windblown sand dunes have formed, usually in association with low-lying areas flanking river estuaries. Thus in St Ives Bay, accumulations occur on either side of the river Hayle, giving rise to the towans of Lelant, Riviere, Mexico, Phillack, Upton and Gwithian, which in places rise to over 70m O.D. Further north-east, and north of Perranporth, lie Gear and Penhale Sands, rising to a height of over 80m O.D., with Holywell just beyond. Other smaller areas of dunes lie near Trevose Head, Padstow and Sennen. They are all the result of strong winds blowing inland across beaches exposed at low tide. Consequently, the sands are highly mobile and, in the past, have submerged buildings and good agricultural land, although they have now been largely stabilised by plantings of Marram Grass (*Ammophila arenaria*). This mobility is caused by the sand, consisting of as much as 60% of comminuted sea shells, which is much lighter than the other main constituent of rounded quartz grains. Consequently the sands themselves, and any soil derived from them, are highly calcareous, and have been used since the reign of Henry III (1216–72) to lighten inland acid soils.

Another feature of these drifting sands is the formation of bars across river estuaries, such as that across the Hayle estuary and the notorious Doom Bar across the Camel. This effect is amplified on the south coast, where the bars have almost completely blocked the outflows of some of the minor rivers, creating inland freshwater lakes, the most noted of which is probably Loe Pool. In time these lakes become choked with sediment, eventually forming marshes, a process which has reached completion at Marazion.

The watershed of the county tends to lie nearer to the north coast than to the south; consequently the south-flowing rivers are longer and usually adopt more sinous courses, in steep-sided wooded valleys and with many tributaries. The systems forming the Tamar and the Fal are by far the largest, although the Fowey and the Helford are not insignificant. The most prominent of the north-flowing rivers are the Hayle and the Camel; but almost every combe or valley opening on to the sea in Cornwall has its own minor stream. All the rivers mentioned have wide estuaries, which are often tidal for considerable distances upstream. Of particular interest are the headwaters of the Fal which rise in Goss Moor, one of a number of lowland mosses in this region; others are Criggan Moors and Red Moor.

SOILS AND VEGETATION

If, as already stated, the geology forms the bones of the county, then the soils and vegetation are the flesh and skin. As already indicated the unimproved natural soils of most of Cornwall are thin, sour, cold and acid; consequently much of the earlier agriculture was confined to the grazing of rough pastures, for which cattle are most suited. As a result, Cornwall became a noted dairy county. Cultivation was limited to groups of small fields, and the boundaries of some of these, probably dating to the Bronze or Iron Ages, can still be seen in places in the Land's End peninsula (Russell 1971), while evidence for cross-ploughing and manuring of this date was found at Gwithian/Godrevy during excavations (Thomas, A.C. 1966).

But it was eventually found that these poor soils, when cleared, drained, and enriched with manure and lime, such as the cretaceous sands from the towans, become extremely fertile. The climate is not entirely suitable for cereals, so that today other crops are grown: potatoes, broccoli, cabbages, and the ubiquitous daffodil, while pastures could be much improved, giving higher yields of milk and meat. Unfortunately, it did not stop with the

A bridleway flanked by Cornish hedges near Hayle.

use of only natural dressings; now, cultivated fields and pastures are drenched with artificial nitrogenous fertilisers and treated with herbicides, insecticides and selective weedkillers, so much so, that in some places up to four crops a year can be taken off them, and the dreaded mono-culture has come to stay. But in this bleak picture, two mitigating factors have remained unchanged: the survival of the Cornish hedge and the multitude, said to number nearly 6,000, of bridleways, footpaths and tracks which criss-cross the county, so that it is unlikely that the fields will ever come to resemble the grain prairies of the eastern counties, where hedges have been grubbed up wholesale.

The thin and acid, untreated soils of lowland Cornwall, of which some few patches still remain, and the corresponding peat-rich soils on the higher area, support an acid-loving flora. The county is comparatively treeless, most deciduous woods being confined to the river valleys of the south coast and their immediate vicinities. Some of the best examples are to be found in the area around Bodmin, where the waters of the south-flowing river Fowey are only separated by just over 6km from the north-flowing Camel, and around the estuaries of the rivers Fal and Tamar. Stands of conifers have been planted in some places on Bodmin Moor. Otherwise trees tend to diminish in numbers towards the west and north of the county, and in many of the areas are confined to hedgerows. Of interest also, and almost unique to Cornwall, are the woods, such as Tehidy Woods, of stunted mature trees, mainly Ash (*Fraxinus excelsior*) and Common Oak (*Quercus robur*), which grow near the north coast. It is thought that, at one time, much of upland Cornwall was covered in similar forests.

Davey (1909) listed over eleven hundred plant species in the county, of which he rated nearly a thousand as native, or aboriginal. This figure has now been revised and updated by French *et al.* (1999). Among the others are those introduced as weeds of cultivation, or by other means, usually associated with man; some of the latter, such as Mesembryanthemum (*Carpobrotus edulis*) and Montbretia (*Crocosmia × crocosmiiflora*), are now well established among indigenous flora. The distribution of native species depends of course on the nature of the soil and its underlying geology. The unimproved moorland vegetation, both at high and low levels, consists largely of mixed heath, interspersed with a variety of grasses, but areas of bracken are often found encroaching, while a scrub of Blackthorn (*Prunus spinosa*), Gorse (*Ulex* spp.) and Brambles (*Rubus* spp.) frequently takes over at lower levels, with Willow (*Salix* spp.) in damper places. The coastal slopes above the sea cliffs are inhabited by similar plant communities, sometimes including Privet (*Ligustrum vulgare*) and Ivy (*Hedera* spp.). Where not encumbered with bracken or scrub, these latter also support a rich and diverse flora, containing Thyme (*Thymus* spp.), Vetches (*Vicia* spp.), Thrift (*Armeria maritima*), Trefoils (*Lotus* spp.), Stonecrops (*Crassula* spp.), Wild Carrot (*Daucus carota*), Sea Campion (*Silene uniflora*), Squill (*Scilla verna*), Betony (*Stachys officinalis*), Red Campion (*Silene dioica*) and Sheep's-bit (*Jasione montana*), with occasional patches of Primrose (*Primula vulgaris*), Violet (*Viola* spp.) and Bluebells (*Hyacinthoides non-scripta*), among others. Many of these plants provide larval foodplants for butterflies, as well as nectar sources for adults.

Of a completely different nature are the calcareous sand dunes, which support communities of lime-loving plants in great variety. Here the Cranesbills (*Geranium* spp.) and other small geraniums are found in abundance, together with occasional

Cowslips (*Primula veris*) and Viper's-bugloss (*Echium vulgare*). The most important plant though is Marram Grass (*Ammophila arenaria*), whose roots are responsible for stabilising the sand, although it is absent from the fixed dunes, having been swamped out by other plants. Near the coastal margins, Sea Holly (*Eryngium maritimum*), Sea Spurge (*Euphorbia paralias*) and Sea Bindweed (*Calystegia soldanella*) grow in almost unadulterated sand, while further

Coastal heathland between Gwennap Head and Carn Guthensbrâs.

inland there is a mass of mainly small species such as Common Centaury (*Centaurium erythraea*), Milkwort (*Polygala vulgaris*), Scarlet Pimpernel (*Anagallis arvensis* ssp. *arvensis*), Speedwells (*Veronica* spp.), Thyme (*Thymus* spp.), Vetches (*Vicia* spp.), Eyebright (*Euphrasia* agg.), Trefoils (*Lotus* spp.), Chickweeds (*Stellaria* spp.) and Early Forget-me-not (*Myosotis ramosissima*); larger plants include Knapweeds (*Centaurea* spp.), Ragwort (*Senecio* spp.), Thistles (*Cirsium* spp.), Hawkweeds (*Pilosella* spp.) and Hawkbits (*Leontodon* spp.) which have probably invaded from further inland. There are also occasional patches of Violets (*Viola* spp.) and Wild Strawberry (*Fragaria vesca*). Scrub, when it occurs is usually made up of the ubiquitous Blackthorn (*Prunus spinosa*) and Gorse (*Ulex* spp.), with Willow (*Salix* spp.), Brambles (*Rubus* spp.), Ivy (*Hedera* spp.), Privet (*Ligustrum vulgare*) and Old Man's Beard (*Clematis vitalba*) interlaced: rarer, but becoming increasingly common, are thickets of Sea Buckthorn (*Hippophae rhamnoides*).

Throughout Cornwall, in addition to river and stream valleys, there are frequent damp and marshy patches on both acid soils and calcareous dunes; they can be found at any height above sea-level, and are caused by natural drainage channels becoming blocked with sediment and silt. In some of the pools and wetter areas, Wild Celery (*Apium graveolens*) is a striking plant, but Bulrushes (*Typha latifolia*), other Rushes (*Juncus* spp.) and Yellow Irises (*Iris pseudacorus*) also occur, while on the surrounding margins and in the damp places are Lady's Smock (*Cardamine pratensis*), the important Devil's-bit Scabious (*Succisa pratensis*) and Hemp Agrimony (*Eupatorium cannabinum*).

Lastly, Cornish hedges, as already indicated, are sufficiently important to warrant a special mention (Menneer 1994). Not only do they provide a sheltered environment, but also a multitude of plants, including many native species as well as weeds of cultivation, which are attractive to butterflies. For instance, some hedges near Connor Downs provide habitats for eighteen resident and two regular migrant species. They also provide, together with footpaths and bridleways, thin corridors of communication, by which the species can spread, and are probably the single most important reason why many butterflies, which are not confined to tight colonies, have been able to hold their own in Cornwall.

CLIMATE

Many people often complain that Cornwall is seldom mentioned in national weather forecasts, and is usually included, if at all, in a general omnibus section called 'the south-west', a term which also embraces Wiltshire. This is not surprising: he would be a rash man to sit in the meteorological offices at Bracknell (Berkshire) and say what is happening to the weather in Cornwall, let alone forecast for the following day, except in the most general terms, when, for instance, the south coast could be shrouded in thick fog and drizzle, while the north coast is basking in brilliant sunshine. Equally, it can be raining in the east of the county, while the west is enjoying sunshine, and vice versa.

Average daily hours of sunshine in July from 1961–90.

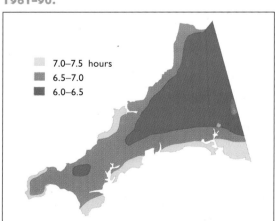

7.0–7.5 hours
6.5–7.0
6.0–6.5

Mean annual rainfall (mm).

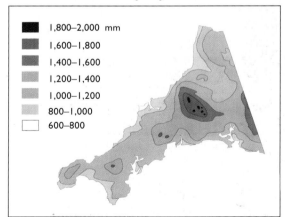

1,800–2,000 mm
1,600–1,800
1,400–1,600
1,200–1,400
1,000–1,200
800–1,000
600–800

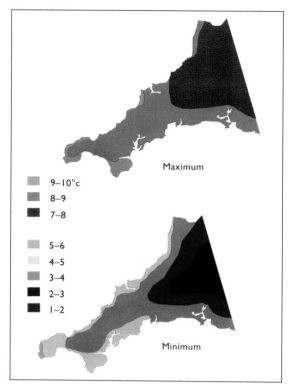

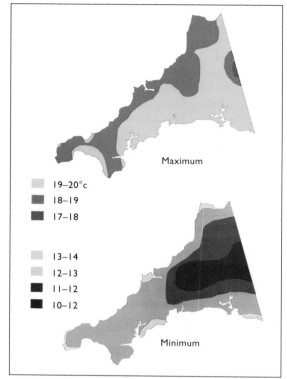

Mean maximum and minimum day temperatures in January from 1961–90.

Mean maximum and minimum day temperatures in July from 1961–90.

The shape and position of Cornwall, in relation to the rest of the country, means that the weather experienced is dependant on many factors; indeed it is probably true to say that no one consistent pattern applies to the whole of the county at one time, and in effect there is a series of rapidly-changing micro-climates for each and every part. Some of the factors involved are: 1) closeness to the coast; 2) sea temperature; 3) height above sea level; 4) general geographical situation; 5) wind direction; 6) air and land temperature; 7) state of the tide. The variations can perhaps be best illustrated by taking three examples.

On a hot summer's day, at dead low water, the exposed sands round the coast heat up. When the tide turns, colder water rapidly invades those sands, often causing a sea fog, and possibly even drizzle, to develop which, as the wind is usually on-shore in hot weather, will be blown inland, only to be dispersed as it passes over warmer ground. Another example depends on the fact that moisture-laden air cools and forms clouds when forced to rise over a high land mass, eventually causing precipitation; consequently, when the wind is blowing from the west or south-west, there is often a narrow strip of the west coast, particularly around Gwennap Head, which is still sunny, when the rest of the county is covered by heavy rain, since there has been neither space nor time in this strip for cloud formation. Indeed, many coastal areas enjoy more sunshine than inland. The third example can also occur in hot dry weather, when, by midday, on-shore breezes have usually risen. But with little more than 30km between north and south coasts at the county's widest, and as little as 9km between St Ives Bay and Mount's Bay, these opposing breezes not only warm and rise (and cool in rising) when they pass over the land, but also collide roughly on the median line of the county, forcing them still higher; the consequence is cloud formation, usually broken, along this line in the middle of the day.

These three examples show how it is almost impossible to predict the weather with any certainty at any given time for much of Cornwall. But that said, there are some generalities that can be made about the climate. Rainfall is high, and falls on about half to two-thirds of the days of the year; there are very few completely windless days, for even in the best weather, sea breezes set in. But that is compensated for by there being little frost, especially in the west of the county and seldom of any severity. For instance, at one place near Hayle, only thirteen days in the winter of 1999–2000 recorded a ground frost, and on only five of those days was very thin ice noted. But quite exceptional was the winter of 1996–97, when over 10cm of ice was formed in one period, due largely to a continuous freezing wind blowing from the north-east for several days. Snow, away from the high moors, occurs only very occasionally, perhaps on average once a decade. With the moderating influence of the sea on all but one side, extremes of temperature, both in summer and winter, are rare.

HABITAT

Putting all the foregoing together produces habitats for butterflies. While many of the commoner species are not particular in their likes or dislikes of habitat – a single farm-track with its hedges can attract over a third of British species – some are much more selective. To this category belong most of the rarer butterflies of Cornwall; it is now realised that the correct management of their habitats is essential for the success or failure in maintaining the species. Unfortunately there are contradictions: bracken is essential for some fritillaries, but it is anathema to the Silver-studded Blue, so a balance would have to be sought, should these species occur in juxtaposition.

The survival of any species of butterfly depends on the presence of a suitable larval foodplant. Some butterflies are again very selective, utilising only one type of plant, while others have been known to lay eggs on as many as 30 different, but related, plant species; consequently it is pointless looking for the Marsh Fritillary (p. 99) unless Devil's-bit Scabious (*Succisa pratensis*) is growing in the area, or for the Grizzled Skipper (p. 25) in the absence of Wild Strawberry (*Fragaria vesca*) or its near relatives. Yet the Orange-tip (p. 44) is quite happy to lay its eggs on almost any cruciferous plant to be found growing in hedgerows and ditches, although a preference for one or two species is usually shown.

But the presence of a suitable larval foodplant is not the only criterion to be observed; its situation is all important. Thus, although Devil's-bit Scabious is necessary for the Marsh Fritillary, the plants need to be in a warm sunny position and standing up well from the surrounding vegetation, which itself must be neither too short nor too long; overgrazing will rapidly extinguish a colony of butterflies, as will complete lack of grazing, when the Scabious is swamped by taller vegetation.

Similarly the caterpillars of several fritillaries feed on the Common Dog-violet (*Viola riviniana*), but again the situation of the plants is vital, and conditions that might suit one will not do for others. For instance, the Dark Green (p. 95) and Small Pearl-bordered (p. 87) Fritillaries delight in warm, open grassland where violets grow in profusion, or, in the case of the latter, in coppiced woodland of three or four years regeneration, where growth has still not extinguished light and warmth, and where violets grow in lush clumps. But the High Brown (p. 92) and Pearl-bordered (p. 89) Fritillaries require very different conditions. The former is highly specific, requiring recent coppicing of only one or two years regeneration, in which a sparse growth of bracken has taken place, to provide also some dead litter; curiously the eggs are not laid on the violet plants but on nearby ground-level dead leaves or twigs. The Pearl-bordered Fritillary can tolerate slightly more mature, regenerating coppice, but probably not so advanced as that which the Small Pearl-bordered can accept. But the Silver-washed Fritillary (p. 97) is quite happy in mature woodland so long as the canopy is reasonably open, and there are plenty of clearings and rides; as with the High Brown Fritillary, the eggs are not laid on the foodplant, but in the crevices of the bark of trees or on dead bracken.

A typical fritillary site at Bunny's Hill.

So it can be seen that although these four fritillaries share a common larval foodplant, each requires a specific and slightly different habitat. Except for the Dark Green Fritillary, these habitats are usually ephemeral, being formed in the process of coppicing woodland and lasting for no more than a year or two before regeneration renders them unsuitable. Any interruption in the coppicing cycle will therefore cause decline, if not extinction of the species.

Habitat can also include other factors apart from vegetation. One family of butterflies, the Lycaenidae, are extremely attractive to ants during their early stages of development. The caterpillar and the chrysalis produce a sweet secretion, often known as 'honeydew', from glands on their bodies, which is 'milked' by the ants; in the absence of ants to remove this liquid, the caterpillars are known to grow mould and die. Frequently the larvae are dragged by the ants into the nests, and in at least one case, the Large Blue caterpillar (p. 69) rewards its hosts by feeding on ant grubs. Many of the blues, the coppers and the hairstreaks are known to have a relationship with ants, but unfortunately for most, the degree of involvement has never been properly worked out; only with the Large Blue has this been extensively studied and elucidated, and there is little doubt that the ants not only extract food, but also protect the larvae from predators. One other butterfly larva, that of the Orange-tip (p. 44), is also said to be attractive to ants.

Several species of ant are involved in these relationships: the wood ant (*Formica rufa*), the red ants (*Myrmica scabrinodis, M. sabuleti* and *M. ruginodis*), the black ants (*Lasius niger* and *L. alienus*), and the yellow ant (*Lasius flavius*). Some butterfly larvae are particular in their association, attracting only one ant species, while others may be attended by several. Consequently, the habitat not only has to contain the right larval foodplant, in an appropriate situation, but has to be one where the relevant ant species is present and can survive as well.

So it can be seen that the creation of the correct habitat for a butterfly is the sum of a complex series of interlocking factors embracing soil type and moisture levels, and the underlying geology, vegetation and its situation, extent of grazing or coppicing, and ground and air temperatures, with other climatic elements. As a result, butterflies are probably one of the best ecological indicators. Most are comparatively easy to identify and highly sensitive to their surroundings, changes in which can cause wild fluctuations in populations.

CHAPTER 3

THE CONSERVATION OF BUTTERFLIES IN CORNWALL

The conservation of butterflies in Cornwall is undertaken by a large number of organisations, farmers, conservationists and private individuals, working alone or together to ensure the survival of rare and common species in gardens and farms, on nature reserves, roadside verges, common land, coastal cliff, sand dune, woodland, moorland and former industrial land. Conservation organisations which manage part of their land holdings for butterflies include: the National Trust, who probably own more high quality butterfly habitat than any other organisation in Cornwall; English Nature, who manage two national nature reserves for butterflies; the Cornwall Wildlife Trust, who manage several nature reserves at least partly for butterflies; the Devon Wildlife Trust, who manage the reserve at Welcombe and Marsland, and even the CBWPS, the Cornwall Bird Watching and Preservation Society, which jointly manage a reserve with the Cornwall Wildlife Trust for the Marsh Fritillary (Table 1). Organisations less obviously associated with nature conservation also play an important part in butterfly conservation: the Ministry of Defence manage their extensive land holdings at Penhale Dunes for rare species including the Silver-studded Blue, and the Duchy of Cornwall manage part of their extensive woodlands for the Heath Fritillary. Many farmers and private individuals also have an important role in nature conservation; without their work, many butterfly species would be restricted to nature reserves and no longer be seen in the wider countryside. As an example, three farmers and landowners are working on the north coast of Cornwall to bring back the Large Blue to their properties; all are putting their own time and money into this project. Even the gardener can provide useful adult nectar sources and larval habitats for many of the more common species.

Many organisations are able to provide advice on habitat management for butterflies. Farmers may receive advice from the Rural Development Service of DEFRA, English Nature and FWAG (the Farming and Wildlife Advisory Group). In particular, DEFRA provides funding to farmers for projects that are beneficial to wildlife, including butterflies; recent government initiatives have allowed DEFRA to be more proactive in gearing Countryside Stewardship schemes to include management for rarities, and these schemes are crucial in the conservation of species such as the Large Blue and the Pearl-bordered Fritillary. English Nature are keen to provide advice on management for butterflies on SSSIs (Sites of Special Scientific Interest) and in SACs (Special Areas of Conservation). It is their policy that all sites with Large Blues should be notified as SSSIs and they are planning to notify the Goss Moor-Breney Common nature reserve complex as a SAC because of the presence of Marsh Fritillary. In connection with this, they are currently funding a project to provide advice on the appropriate mitigation for Marsh Fritillary on the proposed A30 Bodmin to Indian Queens road improvement scheme. In addition, organisations and private individuals may obtain advice from the national office and local branch of Butterfly Conservation.

Much can be achieved through partnership, provided that one partner does not try to claim all the credit for success. In Cornwall, organisations and individual specialists generally work well together. As an example, the Cornwall Biodiversity Initiative was started in 1996 as a partnership between the major conservation bodies in Cornwall with the aim of highlighting the importance of biodiversity as an integral part of our quality of life; as such, biodiversity should be of concern not just to conservationists but to planners, developers, businessmen and the general public. Cornwall Butterfly Conservation played a key part in this process and contributed to the formation of action plans for High Brown Fritillary, Pearl-bordered Fritillary, Marsh Fritillary, Heath Fritillary and Large Blue (Cornwall Biodiversity Initiative 1998). These plans followed the format established by the UK Steering Group and were published in 1995 (UK Steering Group Report 1995). The Cornwall Biodiversity Initiative is currently (2002) revisiting these plans and updating them in the light of recent conservation initiatives; a local action plan is being written for the Silver-studded Blue for which a national action plan was published in 1999 (UK Biodiversity Group 1999).

More closely directed at butterflies is the Cornwall Fritillary Group, chaired by Tim Dingle of North Cornwall District Council, with representatives from Butterfly Conservation, English Nature, Cornwall Wildlife Trust, the National Trust and DEFRA. As its name suggests, this group concentrates on the fritillaries, with the aim of exchanging information, highlighting what needs to be done, co-ordinating conservation work and raising funds. It advised on and directed the re-introduction programme for High

Brown Fritillary, already started by Cornwall Butterfly Conservation. More recently, it raised funding and co-ordinated survey and research work on the Pearl-bordered Fritillary, with matched funding provided by key members putting in their time free of charge. The group is now considering what needs to be done to ensure the long-term survival of the Heath Fritillary in Cornwall.

In addition to these initiatives, there is one organisation which works for the conservation of a single butterfly. The Joint Committee for the Re-establishment of the Large Blue Butterfly is formed from representatives of Butterfly Conservation, the Centre for Ecology and Hydrology, Gloucestershire Wildlife Trust, English Nature, the National Trust and Somerset Wildlife Trust. This committee is active throughout the south-west, including the north Atlantic coast of Cornwall and Devon, and provides specialist scientific advice on habitat management to landowners and conservation organisations, monitors site suitability for re-introductions and manages re-introductions of Large Blue butterflies, mainly by putting down larvae. Two small sub-committees have been formed, one for the successful re-introduction site near Tintagel, one for the group of potential sites on the Devon-Cornwall border. This re-introduction programme shows how much can be achieved by partnerships, especially between conservation organisations and private landowners. In addition, the Eden Project has now begun propagating Wild Thyme for replanting at potential re-introduction sites in Cornwall.

To aid these organisations in the provision of advice, Butterfly Conservation has published their Regional Action Plan for Cornwall, Devon and Somerset (Spalding with Bourn 2000). This plan aims to identify the butterfly and moth species most at risk within the region, to outline the site and management requirements of these species, to identify the most important areas and sites for butterflies and moths and to highlight further survey, management or monitoring work required. The Plan is designed to provide the other partners working for butterflies with detailed conservation priorities for Lepidoptera in Cornwall, in particular to inform action within the Cornwall Biodiversity Initiative. As part of this process, the butterfly species found in Cornwall have been identified as High, Medium and Low Priority, taken from the national classification prepared by Butterfly Conservation (Bourn *et al*. 1996) with some modification for regional differences.

The Regional Action Plan (Spalding with Bourn 2000) identifies the key threats to butterflies in Cornwall. For example, in Cornwall, as elsewhere, there are problems with the isolation of colonies in a fragmented landscape, with the result that natural re-colonisation is not possible when local extinctions occur. Isolation is a real threat to colonies of Silver-studded Blue, Marsh Fritillary, Heath Fritillary and Dingy Skipper and will become a problem for the re-introduced colonies of Large Blue. In addition, the extinction in Cornwall of the High Brown Fritillary may be at least partly due to the breakdown of metapopulation structures as a result of habitat fragmentation. Over-grazing, under-grazing and scrub encroachment (e.g. by European Gorse and Willow) have been identified as some of the main threats to butterflies such as Pearl-bordered Fritillary, High Brown Fritillary, Marsh Fritillary,

Table I. Some nature reserves of major importance for butterflies in Cornwall.

Name	Key butterfly species	Organisation
A site near Tintagel	Large Blue	National Trust
Breney Common	Marsh Fritillary, Silver-studded Blue	Cornwall Wildlife Trust
Goss and Tregoss Moor	Marsh Fritillary, Silver-studded Blue	English Nature
Greenscombe Wood, Luckett	Heath Fritillary	Duchy of Cornwall
Kynance Cove	Silver-studded Blue	National Trust
The Lizard NNR	Marsh Fritillary	English Nature
Penhale Dunes	Silver-studded Blue	Ministry of Defence; Cornwall County Council
Upton Towans	Silver-studded Blue	Cornwall Wildlife Trust; Cornwall County Council
Welcombe and Marsland	High Brown Fritillary, Pearl-bordered Fritillary	Devon Wildlife Trust
Windmill Farm	Marsh Fritillary	Cornwall Bird Watching and Preservation Society; Cornwall Wildlife Trust

Table 2. Suggested actions and targets by Butterfly Conservation for High and Medium Priority species in Cornwall.

	Butterfly	Suggested actions and targets
HIGH PRIORITY BUTTERFLIES	Wood White	Identify all colonies in Cornwall; Consider a programme of re-introduction to old sites in north Cornwall.
	Brown Hairstreak	Survey under-recorded areas to establish true status in north Cornwall.
	Silver-studded Blue	Identify all colonies in Cornwall; Work to ensure survival of small colonies on isolated sites by encouraging suitable management; Restore populations to former sites occupied post-1970, using re-introductions if necessary.
	Large Blue	Assist in re-introduction to a range of sites on the north Atlantic coast.
	Pearl-bordered Fritillary	Work towards the restoration of suitable habitats throughout the butterfly's former range within coastal grasslands and woodland valleys in west Cornwall, the north coast, south-east Cornwall and the fringes of Bodmin Moor; Survey all potential sites; Survey west Cornwall for potential sites and re-introduce to one site if no colonies are found; Establish regular monitoring on seven of the largest sites throughout the region; Raise awareness of the importance of bracken habitats.
	High Brown Fritillary	Seek the restoration of favourable management to former and potential sites including the Seaton Valley LNR, the Woodland Trust reserve at Cancleave, the Tidna and sites on the fringes of Bodmin Moor. If suitable habitat can be restored, it is hoped to introduce the butterfly to at least two sites in Cornwall.
	Marsh Fritillary	Re-survey all previous and present sites to establish status; Acquire one site in Cornwall as a BC nature reserve; Encourage suitable habitat management adjacent to occupied sites; Monitor populations of associated parasitic wasp *Cotesia* spp; Establish habitat association with Double Line moth.
	Heath Fritillary	Re-introduce to former site at Herodsfoot in Cornwall.
MEDIUM PRIORITY BUTTERFLIES	Dingy Skipper	Survey sites with previous records and sites with suitable habitat; Identify the three largest colonies in Cornwall and assess management requirements.
	Grizzled Skipper	Work to protect some surviving colonies by scrub clearance where necessary; Obtain detailed information on the ecology of this species, including the preferred larval foodplants.
	White-letter Hairstreak	Continue to survey areas with significant Wych Elm populations; Encourage planting of resistant elm varieties in suitable areas and the coppicing of diseased Elm.
	Small Pearl-bordered Fritillary	Include in agri-environment agreement schemes; Encourage restoration of suitable habitat where there is potential for re-establishing a network of populations; Establish the ecological requirements of the coastal populations.
	Silver-washed Fritillary	Survey under-recorded areas, especially in west Cornwall.
	Marbled White	Continue to monitor changes in distribution.
	Grayling	Protect abandoned metalliferous mine sites in Cornwall.

Dingy Skipper, Grizzled Skipper, Small Pearl-bordered Fritillary, Marbled White and Grayling. Afforestation, especially with conifers, has been a problem in the past, particularly for Grizzled Skipper, Pearl-bordered Fritillary, High Brown Fritillary and Heath Fritillary, but is probably no longer a major threat. The agricultural improvement of wetlands has contributed to the decline of the Marsh Fritillary and to a lesser extent the Small Pearl-bordered Fritillary. The Grayling has declined inland due to the reclamation of post-industrial sites with the subsequent loss of bare ground habitat and associated short turf grassland.

Many butterflies are being regularly monitored in Cornwall, either through targeted surveys or by means of general butterfly transects. Transects are regularly walked at Bodmin Beacon, Deer Park Wood, Gear Sands, Greenscombe Wood (Luckett) and Gwithian Green. In addition, detailed counts and surveys have taken place for High Brown Fritillary, Pearl-bordered Fritillary, Silver-studded Blue and Marsh Fritillary.

This information has allowed Butterfly Conservation to prepare a list of key actions and targets for the High and Medium Priority butterflies (Spalding with Bourn 2000), summarised in Table 2. One of the main suggested actions is increased survey work, especially for Wood White, Brown Hairstreak, Pearl-bordered Fritillary and Marsh Fritillary, to ensure that all extant colonies are known. For some species, re-introductions are suggested following suitable habitat management and in accordance with Butterfly Conservation's policy on re-introductions. Although some of the plans appear to be ambitious, they help focus action, especially by volunteers, and bring a sense of achievement when targets are realised. Many of the actions proposed in 2000 are now underway in 2002. We now understand much more about butterfly ecology and habitat requirements in Cornwall and can manage nature reserves in a focused way for key species rather than managing in a non-specific way which so often leads to the local extinction of rare species. The Large Blue re-introduction programme is an excellent example of what can be achieved by science-led targeted management that benefits a range of species such as plants, birds, mammals and invertebrates, that occupy the same biotope as the Large Blue. There is now real hope that, after several years of decline, butterfly populations in Cornwall will increase again.

CHAPTER 4

SPECIES ACCOUNTS

HESPERIIDAE
Small Skipper; Essex Skipper; Lulworth Skipper; Large Skipper; Dingy Skipper; Grizzled Skipper

PIERIDAE
Wood White; Pale Clouded Yellow; Berger's Clouded Yellow; Clouded Yellow; Brimstone; Large White; Small White; Green-veined White; Bath White; Orange-tip

LYCAENIDAE
Green Hairstreak; Brown Hairstreak; Purple Hairstreak; White-letter Hairstreak; Small Copper; Long-tailed Blue; Small Blue; Short-tailed Blue; Silver-studded Blue; Brown Argus; Common Blue; Holly Blue; Large Blue

NYMPHALIDAE
White Admiral; Red Admiral; Painted Lady; Small Tortoiseshell; Large Tortoiseshell; Camberwell Beauty; Peacock; Comma; Small Pearl-bordered Fritillary; Pearl-bordered Fritillary; Queen of Spain Fritillary; High Brown Fritillary; Dark Green Fritillary; Silver-washed Fritillary; Marsh Fritillary; Heath Fritillary

SATYRINAE
Speckled Wood; Wall; Marbled White; Grayling; Gatekeeper; Meadow Brown; Ringlet; Small Heath

DANAINAE
Monarch

HESPERIIDAE

Small Skipper *Thymelicus sylvestris*

No. of tetrads (1995–2000): 190
Status in Cornwall: resident
Regional priority: none
Regional rate of change: increasing, +16%

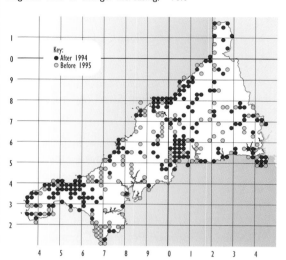

Key:
● After 1994
○ Before 1995

DISTRIBUTION IN CORNWALL

The Small Skipper is widespread but patchy in its distribution in Cornwall and is probably under-recorded due to its small size and habit of flying and basking among tall grasses.

It lives in fairly compact colonies; the largest of these is probably at Gear Sands, Perranporth, where about 2,000 specimens were recorded on two separate occasions in July 1999. Other large colonies inhabit the Towans between Hayle and Gwithian, and Breney Common and Red Moor nature reserves. There are also many records from coastal grasslands, disused mine sites and gardens. The arrival of 15 specimens on a building site in St Austell town centre in July 2000 was something of a surprise, since it is a sedentary species, seldom travelling more than 100–200m.

HABITAT AND ECOLOGY

The butterfly is to be found generally on rough, unimproved grassland; roadside verges and field margins are sufficient to support colonies. It is a robust little butterfly and a strong flyer, and does not seem to mind moderately windy places.

The eggs have been recorded in Cornwall between 15 July and 25 August, but there are apparently no records from the county of the loose tents spun among leaves at the base of the foodplant, in which the pupae overwinter.

The species is single-brooded and has been seen in the county as early as the beginning of June, although many do not normally appear until the end of that month or early July. Numbers begin to decline in early August, with the last specimens surviving until the first week of September.

The adults nectar on Common Ragwort (*Senecio jacobaea*), and other composite flowers, Bell Heather (*Erica cinerea*) and on the rare Heath Lobelia (*Lobelia urens*) which is only found at the Redlake Nature Reserve.

CAUSES OF DECLINE OR INCREASE

During the late nineteenth and early twentieth centuries the Small Skipper was often described as common in Cornwall.

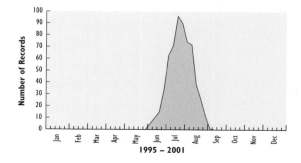

1995 – 2001

Although there is no numerical evidence for a decline, it is probable that many colonies have been lost through habitat destruction, overgrazing and changes in the cutting regime of meadows. Now, however, populations seem reasonably stable, but subject to fluctuations.

CONSERVATION

Overgrazing or changes to the cutting regime of fields and roadside verges will result in the loss of eggs and larvae: reseeding of meadows will make the habitat unsuitable for this butterfly. All should be resisted. The recent tidying up and landscaping of disused mine sites does not benefit the Small Skipper, and likewise should only be done in consultation. The largest colonies are either on nature reserves or on the dunes and consequently reasonably safe, since grazing is likely to be light or non-existent. Fortunately, rabbits usually graze short turf, leaving the longer grasses, where this butterfly is mostly found.

LARVAL FOODPLANTS

The only known foodplant so far recorded in Cornwall is Yorkshire Fog (*Holcus lanatus*), but several other grasses are known to have been used elsewhere, such as Timothy (*Phleum pratense*) and Creeping Soft-grass (*Holcus mollis*).

ABERRATIONS

Aberrations are few in this butterfly and mainly confined to the depth of ground colour of the wings. Only two ab. *obscura* have been recorded in Cornwall; one at Gwithian in July 1984, and the other at Cusgarne in August 1997; in these the hindwings have a dark suffusion.

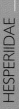

Essex Skipper *Thymelicus lineola*

No. of tetrads (1995–2000): 5
Status in Cornwall: uncertain, possibly resident
Regional priority: low
Regional rate of change: increasing?

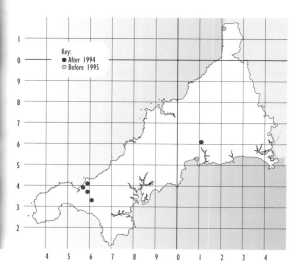

Key:
● After 1994
◐ Before 1995

DISTRIBUTION IN CORNWALL

The marked similarity of this species to the Small Skipper (*T. sylvestris*) has caused a good deal of confusion as to its identification in Cornwall, some reported 'Essex Skippers' turning out, on detailed examination, to be its close relative. It was introduced in 1993 to a private nature reserve at Polscoe near Lostwithiel, where it may survive in very small numbers, but none have been seen since 1995. One was also reported in 1995 at Penhale Sands, but not authenticated; it proved to be a female Small Skipper. Yet the Essex Skipper's northward and westward march in Britain (Asher *et al.* 2001) has been steady if unspectacular and it would be surprising if, sooner or later, it did not occur in increasing numbers in Cornwall. The eggs of this species can apparently be carried in hay (Thomas and Lewington 1991). Cornwall is a noted dairy county, but does not produce much hay: most has to be imported from up-country. The chances then of Essex Skipper eggs sooner of later arriving in the county by this method seem to be very real.

In 1998, a year of abundant Small Skippers in West Cornwall, an attempt was made to see if Essex Skippers were flying unnoticed among them. A large colony of Small Skippers was located on Gwithian Towans on 30 July, of which 43 were netted and marked. Four of these proved to have the unmistakable, sharply-defined black underside to their antennae, the principal characteristic of the Essex Skipper (Wacher 1998a). On extending the search to other sites, a few more were found, notably at Upton Towans. But most gratifying was the discovery of a mating pair at Drannock Lane, Gwinear on 2 August. However, in view of the lack of corroborative evidence, the sightings cannot be confirmed.

Unfortunately, 1999 was a poor year for Skippers generally in West Cornwall and, partly owing to other factors, none were seen at any of these sites; since then the search has not been continued, but would be well worth pursuing at a future date.

HABITAT AND ECOLOGY

The habitat of the adult butterfly is very similar to that of the Small Skipper, and both can often be found flying together in rough uncut grassland on dunes, roadside verges and old mining sites. The Essex Skipper is single brooded with a flight period extending from late June to August, and is generally thought to be slightly later than the Small Skipper. It has provisionally been recorded in Cornwall between mid-July and mid-August, although lack of information prevents greater precision.

CAUSES OF DECLINE OR INCREASE
Suitable habitat exists in many parts of Cornwall, and in view of the national expansion of populations, increase may be expected. Searches should be conducted along the margins of the main roads into the county, and elsewhere in suitable terrain.

CONSERVATION
No conservation of this species is necessary.

LARVAL FOODPLANTS
Although utilising various grasses for foodplants, the Essex Skipper favours different species to the Small Skipper, apparently because they have tighter leaf-sheaths. Thus Cock's-foot (*Dactylis glomerata*) and Creeping Soft-grass (*Holcus mollis*) are known foodplants, while Common-couch (*Elytrigia repens*) and Timothy (*Phleum pratense*) have also been recorded. There are no records of larvae feeding in Cornwall.

ABERRATIONS
Several have been recorded in Britain, but none in Cornwall.

HESPERIIDAE

Lulworth Skipper *Thymelicus acteon*

No. of tetrads (1995–2000): 0
Status in Cornwall: questionable sometime resident?
Regional priority: none
Regional rate of change: now extinct, -100%

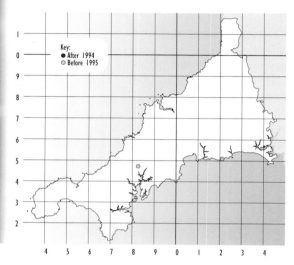

Key:
● After 1994
○ Before 1995

DISTRIBUTION IN CORNWALL

This butterfly's range is now restricted to the coastal fringes of Dorset, centred on Lulworth Cove. It is recorded as having bred in south-east Devon but no adults have been seen there since the late 1960s (Spalding with Bourn 2000). Its existence in Cornwall has always been questionable, although it has been mentioned in the early part of the last century as appearing near Truro and Falmouth (Smith, F.H.N. 1997), which is one of the very few areas in the county where the larval foodplant occurs. A fresh male was supposedly captured near Polperro in 1979 and is now in the Zoological Museum in Amsterdam, but all subsequent attempts to locate the colony, or even further butterflies have failed. If the record is correct, no explanation can be offered for its presence there, unless it was a captive-bred specimen which had been released (see p. 122).

HABITAT

Unimproved grassy downland with a tall growth, mainly on chalk and limestone, or on uncut road and railway verges where chalk and limestone have been used as aggregate. The butterflies seek out south-facing sheltered slopes.

CAUSES OF DECLINE OR INCREASE

Generally by loss of habitat through agricultural development, and in Cornwall probable shortage of larval foodplant (French *et al.* 1999). Note that the latter has disappeared from some of its former sites in the county.

LARVAL FOODPLANT

The only recognised foodplant is tall growing Torgrass (*Brachypodium pinnatum*), which needs to be at least 30cm high. This grass only occurs in Cornwall at three sites around Truro, two on Penhale Sands and one north-east of Bude (French *et al.* 1999).

ABERRATIONS

None have been recorded in the county.

Large Skipper *Ochlodes venata*

No. of tetrads (1995–2000): 194
Status in Cornwall: resident
Regional priority: none
Regional rate of change: increasing, +24%

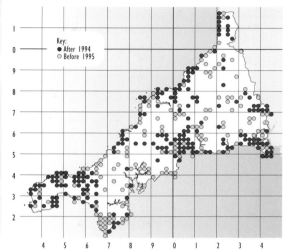

Key:
● After 1994
○ Before 1995

DISTRIBUTION IN CORNWALL
The butterfly is found almost throughout the whole county, although in small numbers. The gaps in the distribution map probably appear as they are, due to colonies being missed because of their small size, and also possibly because there are less recorders inland. The main larval foodplant is absent from the higher ground of Bodmin Moor, which explains the paucity of records there.

HABITAT AND ECOLOGY
The habitat of the Large Skipper is in sheltered areas with long, uncut grass; very small patches of long grass are sufficient to support a colony. Rarely are 30 or more individuals recorded at any one spot, and often there are less than ten. Coastal footpaths seem to be most-favoured in Cornwall, perhaps because there is little grazing, and grass cutting is minimal, if at all. It has also been seen on dunes, at old industrial sites, and in meadows; even the rough grass of a roadside verge is sufficient to support a colony, while it is often a visitor to rural gardens. Although it rests on brambles (*Rubus* spp.), there are no records of it nectaring on these plants, and it is most often observed sunning itself, with wings half-open in the characteristic Skipper attitude, on a blade of grass or other vegetation.

The butterfly is single-brooded and begins to appear in early May. It has a relatively long flight period, and specimens have occurred as late as early September, although July and August are more normal.

CAUSES OF DECLINE OR INCREASE
Many colonies will have been lost with the ploughing and reseeding of meadows with unsuitable grasses, such as Perenial Rye-grass (*Lolium perenne*). But its propensity for surviving in small colonies in restricted areas means that it is holding its own in Cornwall.

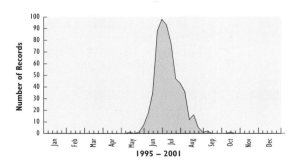

CONSERVATION
In the short term, no management at all is probably the best action for this species; cutting of long grass can destroy three

out of the four stages of development, since all these live at 10–40cm above ground in the stems or leaves. The current practice of leaving the grass verges in lanes and bridleways uncut can only be of benefit to the Large Skipper. In the long term, prevention of shading of these areas by the clearance or trimming of scrub will also be beneficial. Growth of long grass in set-aside fields can temporarily increase numbers (Asher *et al.* 2001), although there is no evidence of this happening in Cornwall.

LARVAL FOODPLANTS

Cock's-foot (*Dactylis glomerata*) is the only foodplant recorded in Cornwall. Purple Moor-grass (*Molinia caerulea*) and False Brome (*Brachypodium sylvaticum*) have both been reported as occasional foodplants elsewhere.

ABERRATIONS

Some aberrations of the Large Skipper are known, but none have been recorded in Cornwall.

Dingy Skipper *Erynnis tages*

No. of tetrads (1995–2000): 26
Status in Cornwall: resident
Regional priority: medium
Regional rate of change: declining, but probably now stabilised, +26%

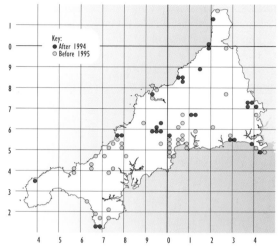

Key:
● After 1994
○ Before 1995

DISTRIBUTION IN CORNWALL

The Dingy Skipper was once locally but fairly widespread through central and east Cornwall, but not in west Penwith and the Lizard. It has now declined considerably in the centre of the county, but new appearances have been reported from near Pendeen in the west and near Kynance in the Lizard; these may represent recently-discovered pre-existent colonies. Elsewhere it continues to hold its own on Penhale and Rock dunes and near Delabole; on the south-east coast there are colonies east of Looe, at Tregantle and near Rame.

Some inland colonies also survive. There is a group around Luckett, another at Bunny's Hill, and a third and larger group around the neighbourhood of Goss Moor. An isolated colony exists at the Marsland Nature Reserve.

HABITAT AND ECOLOGY

The adult butterfly favours well-drained, rough pasture in sheltered, sunny places. In Cornwall this encompasses dunes, old railway lines, disused quarries and industrial sites, and woodland margins wherever larval foodplants grow in a sparse sward, and where there is a mixture of taller vegetation for shelter.

Many colonies are small, producing perhaps no more than 50 adults in any one flight period. Although a rather sedentary species, it is capable of flights up to a few kilometres which enables it to establish new colonies in favourable habitats.

This active little butterfly has one unusual feature. When at rest it resembles a small Noctuid moth with wings outspread and curved back in a position unlike any other British species.

The butterfly is normally on the wing from late April to early June, with a rare second generation appearing in August (Emmet and Heath 1990).

CAUSES OF DECLINE OR INCREASE

The decline in Cornwall has been due almost entirely to the destruction of habitat, with the reclamation of wasteland and

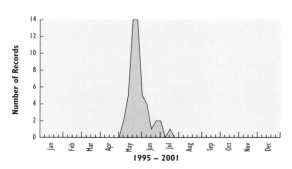

1995 – 2001

its conversion to agriculture or development. Shading out of woodland clearings and overgrazing have played their part in its decline.

CONSERVATION

The colonies at Penhale are probably safe so long as the Ministry of Defence remain in possession of some areas and providing Perransands holiday camp is not enlarged.

The same can be said of the group of colonies at Goss Moor, providing suitable habitats can be maintained by occasional scrub control. Elsewhere, tidying up of old industrial sites should be resisted, although again scrub and bracken control are essential (Spalding with Bourn 2000).

LARVAL FOODPLANTS

The normal foodplant is Common Bird's-foot Trefoil (*Lotus corniculatus*), but Greater Bird's-foot Trefoil (*Lotus pedunculatus*) can be used in damp areas.

ABERRATIONS

Minor variations of colour or markings are comparatively common, although none have been recorded in Cornwall. The scarce second brood is said to have a paler ground colour on both sides of its wings.

Grizzled Skipper *Pyrgus malvae*

No. of tetrads (1995–2000): 7
Status in Cornwall: resident
Regional priority: medium
Regional rate of change: decreasing, but colonies thriving, +42%

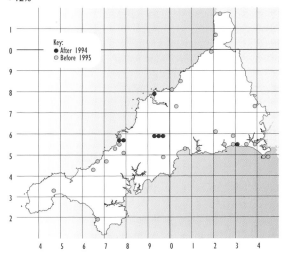

Key:
● After 1994
○ Before 1995

DISTRIBUTION IN CORNWALL

The Grizzled Skipper has declined in recent years in Cornwall, and is now confined perhaps to no more than about three sites; consequently it is one of the county's rarer butterflies. The strongest population is widespread and extends through two tetrads north from Perransands to Penhale, where the adults have been found annually, but seldom in higher numbers than a hundred or so, in every year since at least the 1980s. It is known that the Ministry of Defence land safeguards other colonies within these tetrads.

In contrast, another colony on Goss Moor is much more concentrated on a disused railway line and covers no more than a few hundred square metres; it seems to be dependent on one or two patches of larval food plants, and an estimate of about 50 adults may appear in the flight period. Unfortunately the site is now under threat, since the railway line may be returned to use.

The third colony has been reported on the Cornwall-Devon border at the Marsland nature reserve. The Grizzled Skipper has also been recorded on the dunes near Rock. The last woodland colony in Cornwall at Keveral Wood became extinct in the late 1980s when conifers, planted earlier, matured to shade out the foodplants.

HABITAT AND ECOLOGY

The preferred habitat is a relatively low, sunny sward with occasional low scrub and some undulations in the terrain, and is similar to that required by the Dingy Skipper. Thus, on the dunes, where the foodplants are widespread, it seems to exist in small, discreet colonies, which together cover more than one tetrad. For a small butterfly, although often nectaring, it seems to spend much of its time in sheltered hollows in the dunes, basking with its wings wide open on bare ground or short turf. It is very agile and a rapid flyer which is readily disturbed; so it can easily be missed by the observer.

The males appear to be territorial. Females are seen less often, but become more conspicuous when egg laying. Away from the dunes, it inhabits sheltered but unshaded rides and glades and sunny fringes of woods. The butterfly is normally single brooded in Britain, appearing on the wing in early May,

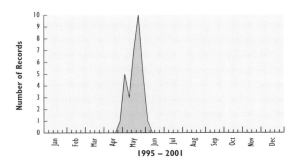

1995 – 2001

with a peak later in the month, and continues until late June. In warm early springs it has been recorded in April, while late specimens in July and August may belong to a partial second generation, which is rare in Britain but regular in southern Europe (Emmet and Heath 1990).

CAUSES OF DECLINE OR INCREASE

With such a low population in the county, it is difficult to monitor fluctuations, but as more and more neglected landscapes, such as disused industrial sites, are tidied up or put to agricultural use, so rough, open sunny areas cease to be available. This, in combination with lack of grazing by stock and rabbits, restricts suitable habitats, while woodland sites can be shaded out by the growth of trees. Annual fluctuations can be caused by the weather, a very wet winter depleting numbers significantly, although recovery can take place during following warmer, drier seasons.

CONSERVATION

The colonies on Penhale and Perransands are probably secure, providing they stay under Ministry of Defence protection, and providing Perransands holiday camp is not allowed to expand northwards. Penhale Dunes is also a Special Area of Conservation, and as such is legally protected.

At Goss Moor much depends on the scheme to replace the railway, although that in itself need not be a threat, since the Grizzled Skipper is quite happy on railway embankments, so long as these are not regularly sprayed; but it would be the concomitant disturbance by the engineering works and related tidying up which is the real danger. It has been suggested that the whole colony may be dug up and relocated to another suitable habitat nearby, but attempts to do this with other species elsewhere have not been altogether successful (Spalding with Bourn 2000).

LARVAL FOODPLANTS

Wild Strawberry (*Fragaria vesca*) is the favoured foodplant, which occurs abundantly in Cornwall. Alternatives are Tormentil (*Potentilla erecta*), Creeping Cinquefoil (*Potentilla reptans*), Agrimony (*Agrimonia eupatoria*), Silverweed (*Potentilla anserina*) and Blackberry (*Rubus fruticosus*).

ABERRATIONS

An extreme form in which the white spots aggregate on the forewings to form white horizontal bars with a reduced number of spots on the hindwings (ab. *taras*), occurs frequently at Penhale and Perransands. It was estimated that between 1989–92 up to 40% of some of the colonies consisted of this form, which has not appeared anywhere else in Cornwall. No other aberrations have been recorded in the county.

Grizzled Skipper, ab. *taras*.

Wood White *Leptidea sinapis*

No. of tetrads (1995–2000): 0
Status in Cornwall: possibly resident only in the north
Regional priority: high
Regional rate of change: 0%

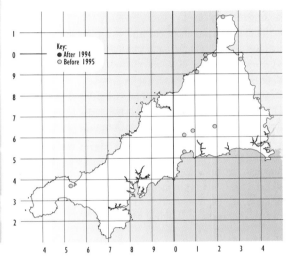

Key:
● After 1994
○ Before 1995

DISTRIBUTION

At best the species may be said to be sparse and local in the county, with few records in the last decade; at worst, it may be virtually extinct as a breeding species. The Wood White is most likely to occur in the northern and eastern parts of the county, to which individuals from the Devon colonies may stray. Recorded sightings, in the 1980s, were mainly in this area, with those at the Marsland nature reserve in June 1989 and 1990; continuing south through Marsland Mouth, Bude, the Valency Valley and Millook single specimens were recorded in 1982, 1985, 1989 and 1990, with two in 1986 (Smith, F.H.N. 1997). Another was seen just north of the Cornwall border in 1993; thus it may still occur in this region, given prolonged northerly winds.

Apparently, though, there are two other areas in the county where the butterfly has been seen in the last two decades. One is in the Lanhydrock-Breney Common region: a single specimen was seen near Lanhydrock (following one in the mid-1960s), two more in 1988 adjacent to the Common and possibly another in the same year at Redlake Reserve, only about 3km south-east, following two to three weeks of northerly winds.

The second area, is surprisingly in the west of the county near St Ives, where a sparse colony seems to have existed in the 1970s and 1980s in woods near Trencrom; unfortunately the habitat has now been destroyed.

HABITAT AND ECOLOGY

Typical habitats are scrubby woodland edges and woodland rides and clearings; the butterfly may also be found on minor roads and tracks, away from woods, which it uses as lines of communication. Its distinctive but weak flight makes identification moderately easy, although it can be confused with the Green-veined White. Any colonies are likely to be where the larval foodplants are abundant, and such were the last-known ones in the coastal and inland valleys of north Cornwall; sites here on scrub land, small woods and country byways should be searched in June.

It is claimed that there is only one brood in Cornwall (Frohawk 1934; Emmet and Heath 1990), although a partial second generation occurs elsewhere in southern Britain. Where there is only one generation, adults are said to emerge in late May and continue until the end of July. This flight pattern would account for a specimen taken in woods near St Austell at the beginning of August 1939 and two others taken east of Bude in late July 1945, and would be in accord with Frohawk (1934) noting that it occurs in July in north Cornwall. But where a partial second brood occurs, the first brood appearances are earlier, lasting from early May until the end of June, with the second occurring from mid-July until late August. Consequently, the specimens captured near

St Austell and Bude, and those referred to by Frohawk, could belong to either generation, and carry the implication that it could be double-brooded in Cornwall.

CAUSES OF DECLINE OR INCREASE

Although never prolific, or even common during the twentieth century in Cornwall, it was considerably more widespread at the end of the nineteenth. The long, slow decline was undoubtedly due to loss of habitat, with inappropriate changes in woodland management leading to loss of glades and fringes, and continuity of open rides (Spalding with Bourn 2000). Cornwall is a county with little woodland and shelter for such a fragile insect. Modern conservation methods may have created favourable habitats, but they are probably too far apart, with no joining corridors, for re-colonisation, other than perhaps in the Stratton and Bude region.

CONSERVATION

It would seem that the re-creation of the Wood White's favoured habitats, in areas which it formerly frequented, such as the Millook and Valency Valleys, might encourage its re-colonisation. This would include some scrub clearance and reinstated grazing, followed possibly by re-introduction from the nearby Devon colonies (Spalding with Bourn 2000).

LARVAL FOODPLANTS

Although the larvae feed on a variety of leguminous plants, Meadow Vetchling (*Lathyrus pratensis*) and Bitter Vetch (*Lathyrus linifolius* var. *montanus*) seem to be most preferred; it should be noted that the latter is commoner in east Cornwall, particularly in the north. Tufted Vetch (*Vicia cracca*), common throughout Cornwall, and Common Bird's-foot Trefoil (*Lotus corniculatus*) can also be used.

ABERRATIONS

Aberrations in this species are few and none have been recorded in Cornwall.

Pale Clouded Yellow *Colias hyale*

No. of tetrads (1995–2000): 4
Status in Cornwall: rare migrant
Regional priority: none
Regional rate of change: variable

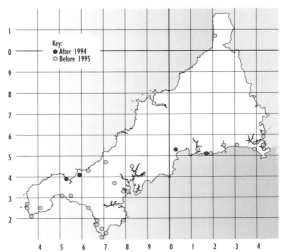

Key:
● After 1994
○ Before 1995

DISTRIBUTION IN CORNWALL

The Pale Clouded Yellow is one of the rare migrants to the county and no more that about 50 sightings have been made since the first record in September 1796 (Penhallurick 1996). Since then, years when more than one adult has been seen (numbers in brackets) have been 1892(3), 1900(2), 1906(8), 1940(?), 1945(5), 1955(8) and 1983(5); single adults were recorded in 1857, 1965, 1968 and 1978. Confusion is caused by the close similarity between this species and *C. croceus* f. *helice* (p. 33) and also Berger's Clouded Yellow (*C. alfacariensis*) (p. 31), which was first recognised as a separate species by the examination of specimens from southern Spain in the Netherlands in 1945 (Berger 1948). Consequently records earlier than that year may have unwittingly included some of the latter species. Correct identification of the Pale Clouded Yellow can only properly be made if the specimen is netted and examined, or it is seen for a protracted period at rest. In more recent years one was seen at Porthgwarra in October 1990, another at Land's End in August 1992; two were seen in 1992, one at Truro in July, the other at Whitesand Bay also in July. Thereafter one was seen in August 1994 near Polperro. In 1996 there was a relative abundance of Clouded Yellows (*C. croceus*) during late July, August and September. Among them on Gwithian Towans in August was a Pale Clouded Yellow; it was a windy day, so it was fairly sedentary and could easily be netted and positively identified as a female. Later, in September a male was netted on the top footpath at Carbis Bay leading from Headland Road to the West Cornwall Golf Course, while a female was observed for quite some time nectaring on *Erigeron* spp. in a nearby garden; since the butterfly always sits with its wings closed, and is difficult to identify from the undersides only, it was also netted (Wacher 1998b). Unfortunately only one was reported in 1998, another good year for Clouded Yellows, at Lanivet in September 1998. Two more were sighted in 2000; one at Holmbush (Lane 2000c), and the other at Perran Downs in September, although the latter was not confirmed.

HABITAT AND ECOLOGY

The Pale Clouded Yellow can be seen almost anywhere, in gardens, along footpaths and lanes, in fields and on dunes, but its favoured habitat is fields with an abundance of foodplants.

The species has not yet been recognised as breeding in Cornwall in the wild, but the caterpillar when fully grown can be clearly distinguished from that of Berger's Clouded Yellow (*C. alfacariensis*).

The species cannot usually survive the British winter in any form. But in 1947, a successful second brood was noted in the wild in Kent, where, after the mild following winter of 1947–48, numerous specimens were seen in the same fields in May 1948, and also in Essex. There is, therefore, a strong presumption of a winter survival, since there was no evidence of early migrant arrivals (Emmet and Heath 1990).

Moreover in Cornwall, a female captured in July 1945, somewhere on the south coast between Longrock and Trewavas Head, laid eggs freely on growing clover (*Trifolium* spp.); all but one of the resulting caterpillars eventually pupated, and the adult butterflies emerged during the first fortnight of September, giving rise to what must have been a third brood.

Normally two broods are known with, in a good year, a partial third brood. Most British immigrants belong to the second brood, and arrive here in July and August, extending on into September, and even late October, although there must remain a suspicion that these late specimens belong to a third generation, which had bred in the county.

CONSERVATION
No conservation of this species is necessary.

LARVAL FOODPLANTS
Either Clover species (*Trifolium* spp.) or Lucerne (*Medicago sativa*), which is rare in Cornwall, are the favoured larval foodplants, but other leguminous species can be used.

ABERRATIONS
Major aberrations are rare and none have been recorded in Cornwall.

Berger's Clouded Yellow *Colias alfacariensis*

No. of tetrads (1995–2000): 0
Status in Cornwall: very rare migrant
Regional priority: none
Regional rate of change: not assessed

DISTRIBUTION IN CORNWALL

A rarer immigrant than the Pale Clouded Yellow (*C. hyale*), only one authenticated specimen has ever been recorded in Cornwall, at Polruan in August 1960. Reference has already been made to the difficulty of distinguishing this butterfly from the Pale Clouded Yellow (*C. hyale*), (p. 29) and some authorities insist that identification can only be made by judging, either a number of characteristics together, or the structure of the genitalia, from captured and set specimens (Emmet and Heath 1990).

HABITAT AND ECOLOGY

In Britain, there is no record of breeding in the wild (see below), and such information as there is comes from rearings in captivity. Fortunately, the caterpillar can easily be distinguished from that of the Pale Clouded Yellow (*C. hyale*) and in maturity is a deep turquoise green in colour with two yellow spiracular stripes; the whole body is covered in short black hairs.

The butterfly is most commonly to be seen in August and September, through to October, the specimens presumably representing the second brood. Some adults recorded in Kent in May 1948 are thought to have been offspring of those seen the previous August, having survived the mild winter of 1947–48 (see p. 29). The butterfly is most commonly seen among its foodplants.

No increase or decline can be recorded.

CONSERVATION

No conservation is necessary for this species.

LARVAL FOODPLANTS

Horseshoe Vetch (*Hippocrepis comosa*) is most favoured, but is not known to occur in Cornwall, being a plant of chalk and limestone areas. The butterfly is said to ignore Lucerne (*Medicago sativa*), the foodplant of the Pale Clouded Yellow (*C. hyale*), but opinion is divided (Emmet and Heath 1990, *contra* Penhallurick 1996). On the continent, it is known to use Crown Vetch (*Securigera varia*), but this is a rare introduction to Cornwall, mostly as a garden escape.

ABERRATIONS

Few aberrations have been noted among British specimens.

Clouded Yellow *Colias croceus*

No. of tetrads (1995–2000): 231
Status in Cornwall: comparatively common migrant
Regional priority: none
Regional rate of change: variable

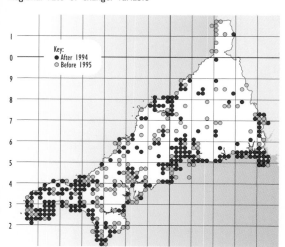

Key:
● After 1994
◉ Before 1995

DISTRIBUTION IN CORNWALL

As an almost annual, if irregular immigrant, the distribution of the Clouded Yellow in Cornwall varies from year to year. Few years go by when it has not been recorded, although in poor years, it may be restricted to two or three tetrads. In good years it is widespread, but is more often to be seen along the prime localities of the south coast. From there it disperses inland, eventually reaching the downs and dunes of the north coast. Total numbers in any one year can vary from ten to 10,000 (as in 1947). Other recent prolific years for the butterfly have been 1996 and 2000.

During summer immigration there is a distinct movement in a north or north-easterly direction, but this is reversed in the late summer and autumn towards the south and west as the later broods attempt to emigrate, since they cannot normally survive the British winter.

HABITAT AND ECOLOGY

The Clouded Yellow can be seen almost anywhere, in fields, gardens, meadows or waste ground. More especially it delights in fields of clover (*Trifolium* spp.) or Lucerne (*Medicago sativa*), or other flower-rich areas with trefoils and vetches. It is a fast, strong flyer and is tolerant of open windy places. When at rest, it almost invariably sits with its wings closed, a habit which can sometimes cause confusion with allied species.

The butterfly is recorded as very occasionally surviving the winter as a caterpillar or pupa near the south coast. These give rise to adults in late March, and are likely to be the earliest seen in any year. The species is continuously brooded in its homelands of north Africa and southern Europe, and the first migrants usually arrive in Cornwall in May or June. These will produce a first British brood in August, which swell the numbers of later migrants; in favourable years there is a second brood in October or later. Indeed, in 1998, not an especially good year, the Clouded Yellow was one of the commonest butterflies in west Cornwall in September and October and one was seen as late as

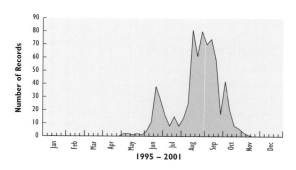

1995 – 2001

17 December near Hayle. Another was even seen near St Austell on Christmas Day 1966! Attempts at a reverse migration in the autumn have already been noted.

CAUSES OF DECLINE OR INCREASE

The wide variation in the numbers reaching Cornwall in different years is most likely caused by the weather systems in Europe and Africa. Those reaching the county relatively early usually produce at least one brood, given reasonably good weather, but a poor, wet summer can rapidly reduce the numbers. Immigration can sometimes be too late for a home brood to reach adult status. Cornwall is fortunate that, even when national numbers are few, it is one of the most advantageous counties in which to witness both immigration and emigration.

CONSERVATION

There is little that can be done to promote this species, but it should be noted that, since clovers are still cultivated, it is one of the few butterflies that can benefit from the modern, farmed countryside, providing spraying with insecticides is controlled.

LARVAL FOODPLANTS

Commonest are various species of Clover (*Trifolium* spp.) both wild and cultivated. Alternatively Lucerne (*Medicago sativa*), Common Bird's-foot Trefoil (*Lotus corniculatus*), other trefoils and vetches can be used.

ABERRATIONS

The male exhibits few aberrations and most occur in the female, of which the commonest has been recognised as a form *helice*. In some years as many as 10% of females can be of this form, and they appear more abundantly in both British broods in August, September and October, although undoubtedly it occurs also in the initial migrants.

Four main aberrations of f. *helice* have been recognised. It most frequently appears in Cornwall with a white (ab. *alba*) or creamy-white ground colour to its wings, and can then be mistaken for a Large White. In the second form the ground colour is flushed with apricot, and specimens have been taken at Gribben Head, near Fowey and at Pentewan Beach, both in 1992.

There is also a pale yellow form, which can be confused with a Pale, or Berger's, Clouded Yellow; an example was caught at St John in 1983. The last type has the wings shot with purple, blue or violet (ab. *purpurascens*) but has not been seen in Cornwall.

Aberrations can occur with normal females, as well as with the types of f. *helice* and are usually associated with the black markings, or with the colour of the discoidal spot on the hindwings, which can vary considerably from deep orange to pale lemon. Also in 1992 at Pentewan a white f. *helice* was captured which was almost devoid of the pale spots in the black borders. Another seen at Bude in 1935 had these same spots enlarged to form a continuous band.

A number of f. *helice* were bred from eggs laid by a first-brood female captured near Lostwithiel in 1994. These produced adults in mid-November, the larvae having been fed on potted clover plants. Two which emerged had no trace of pale spotting in the black borders (ab. *pseudomas*) (Russwurm 1978).

It should also be noted that immigrants almost always have a greater wingspan than British specimens, presumably because they have bred under more favourable conditions.

Clouded Yellow f. *helice* at Well Park, Polscoe, Lostwithiel.

Brimstone *Gonepteryx rhamni*

PIERIDAE

No. of tetrads (1995–2000): 137
Status in Cornwall: resident
Regional priority: none
Regional rate of change: increasing, +25%

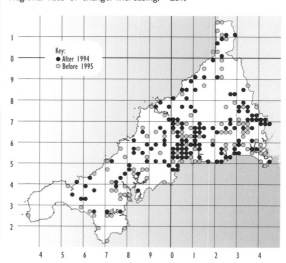

Key:
● After 1994
○ Before 1995

DISTRIBUTION IN CORNWALL

The Brimstone is widespread throughout most of Cornwall, although it is less so west of Truro and is almost entirely absent from the Lizard and west Penwith, due to the lack of a suitable larval foodplant. However, the female especially has a wandering habit and one, a female, was recorded at Upton Towans in April 1997; also a male at St Erth in April 1992, another male at Carbis Bay in May 1990 and, the most westerly, a male near Land's End in 1991, all despite the restrictions caused by the absence of foodplants. The furthest west it breeds would seem to be Godolphin Woods, where specimens are recorded almost every year and where some foodplant grows.

HABITAT AND ECOLOGY

The commonest places to find Brimstone are in woods among evergreens, such as holly and ivy, rather than in the more open spaces that they choose for breeding. But their wandering habit means that they can be met with almost anywhere in woods, hedgerows, scrubby places, fields and even gardens, where they will happily nectar on cultivated flowers. Other favoured nectar plants are Teasel (*Dipsacus fullonum*), Thistles (*Cirsium* spp.) and Knapweed (*Centaurea nigra*). The bluish-green caterpillars are easily found, especially where feeding-damage is detected, but a large number fail to make maturity owing to predation by birds and by the parasitic Tachinid Fly (*Phryxe vulgaris*), which, in Cornwall, is mainly found in coastal regions.

With only one generation a year, the Brimstone is, with the Small Tortoiseshell, one of the longest-lived British butterflies. It overwinters as the adult and is one of the earliest butterflies to appear in the spring, often as early as January in Cornwall (Penhallurick 1996). These adults often live long enough to overlap the next generation, which is on the wing from late July and August. Consequently there is no month of the year when a Brimstone could not be seen.

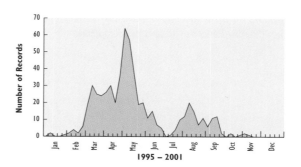

CAUSES OF DECLINE OR INCREASE

The Brimstone seems to be holding its own in Cornwall, and with a supply of appropriate foodplants (see below), may yet extend its range into the far west of the county.

CONSERVATION

Attempts have been made to establish larval foodplants in west Cornwall by the distribution of 200 alder buckthorns, grown from local seed, to a number of people living west of Truro. A small conservation group has also planted 20 of these shrubs in the area of Godolphin Woods, hoping to encourage the resident population in the woods to breed more freely.

LARVAL FOODPLANTS

The principal foodplant is Alder Buckthorn (*Frangula alnus*) which, it has been noted in the *Flora of Cornwall* (French *et al.* 1999), 'has been much planted in various places in west Cornwall to encourage the population of Brimstone Butterflies'. Purging Buckthorn (*Rhamnus cathartica*) has been used as an alternative, but does not occur in Cornwall.

ABERRATIONS

Aberrations of this species are rare and none have been recorded in Cornwall.

Large White *Pieris brassicae*

No. of tetrads (1995–2000): 413
Status in Cornwall: resident and migrant
Regional priority: none
Regional rate of change: stable, with fluctuations caused by migrations, +10%

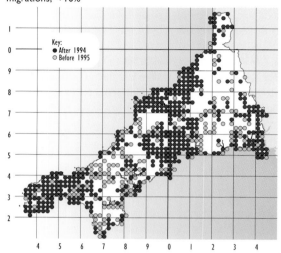

Key:
● After 1994
○ Before 1995

DISTRIBUTION IN CORNWALL

This highly mobile and strong-flying butterfly, often referred to as the 'Cabbage White', can be seen anywhere in Cornwall, even occasionally on the higher moors, but it is most frequently to be observed in the region of broccoli and cabbage fields, which now proliferate in the county; it is also a common visitor to gardens and appears in urban areas. Elsewhere it is said to be attracted to Oil-seed Rape (*Brassica napus*) although there is little of that in Cornwall.

The distribution map presents some puzzles, since it shows two areas where, in the last five years fewer have been recorded. Admittedly that in the east of the county includes Bodmin Moor, where they would not be expected to be so common, as in the much smaller one representing the high moors of west Penwith, but no such reason can be advanced for the large area stretching north from the Lizard; indeed being a migrant a greater abundance might be expected around the Lizard itself. Consequently, the map suffers from the main deficiency of distribution maps and gives a slightly false impression, representing the distribution of observers, not of the butterfly.

HABITAT AND ECOLOGY

As noted above, the Large White can be found almost anywhere, more especially where larval foodplants are abundant, or there are good nectar sources. The butterfly is very fond of the flowers of certain Compositae, such as Knapweed (*Centaurea nigra*) and varieties of thistle.

The butterfly has two main broods a year, with a partial third brood in Cornwall. Since it overwinters as a chrysalis, the first brood can occur exceptionally early in the county, often in March, with occasional specimens being recorded in February, but normally significant numbers do not appear until the second week of April. The second brood emerges from July onwards into August and September and is much more numerous than the first. But by then numbers have been inflated by migrants, which fluctuate from year to year. These start their own breeding cycle which may not be in phase with the home specimens;

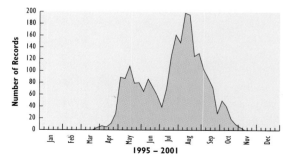

1995 – 2001

consequently it is often possible to find all four stages of the life-cycle at the same time. Very large immigrations of Large Whites have been recorded from Cornwall, most recently in 1986 and 1988 (Penhallurick 1996). It is not thought though that these mass migrations have had much influence on overall numbers in recent years (Asher *et al*. 2001). Specimens of the butterfly seen in October and even November may be the progeny of late migrants or of a partial third brood of residents. There is also some evidence to show that a reverse migration occurs in late summer and early autumn (Asher *et al*. 2001).

CAUSES OF DECLINE OR INCREASE

As already noted, numbers of this butterfly fluctuate from year to year. In the past, they often reached epidemic proportions, seriously damaging crops, but, with the advent of modern insecticides, similar depredations are now unlikely to happen. Parasitic infestation of caterpillars by the wasp *Apanteles glomeratus* can also occur, and it has been reckoned that mortality rates of larvae can be as high as 95% (Asher *et al*. 2001), an important factor in the natural control of the species, which if uncontrolled can become a serious pest.

CONSERVATION

No conservation of this species is necessary.

LARVAL FOODPLANTS

The larvae feed on many species of the Cruciferae family, both wild and cultivated, although they show a preference for the latter; it is not thought that wild species are important (Asher *et al*. 2001). Consequently, they are well provided for in Cornwall with its abundance of cabbage, various types of broccoli and cauliflower, spring greens and other brassicas. They will also feed on garden plants such as Nasturtium (*Tropaeolum majus*), Wallflowers (*Erysium cheiri*), Virginia Stocks (*Malcolmia maritima*) and Honesty (*Lunaria annua*), which is now naturalised as a garden escape in much of Cornwall. Indeed there is a record of a crop of Honesty grown for the market near Penzance in the late nineteenth century which was much damaged by the larvae (Penhallurick 1996). Near the coast they will utilise Seakale (*Crambe maritima*) and Wild Mignonette (*Reseda lutea*) both of which occur in the county, but less commonly than other foodplants. Larvae have also been observed on Horseradish (*Armoracia rusticana*) in a garden near Hayle.

ABERRATIONS

Although aberrations are uncommon in the Large White, some occasionally occur, mainly involving the black markings on the wings, but none have been recorded in Cornwall. It may be that the butterfly is so common that insufficient attention has been paid to identify specific aberrations. There is, however, evidence of seasonal dimorphism, with the black markings of the spring specimens being dusted over with grey scales (Emmet and Heath 1990).

Small White *Pieris rapae*

PIERIDAE

No. of tetrads (1995–2000): 435
Status in Cornwall: resident and migrant
Regional priority: none
Regional rate of change: increasing, but less so than formerly, +14%

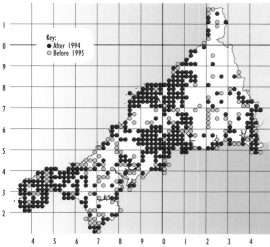

Key:
● After 1994
○ Before 1995

DISTRIBUTION IN CORNWALL

As with its near relative the Large White, this butterfly is popularly included in the term 'Cabbage White'. Its distribution in Cornwall is similar and once again probably reflects the density of observers rather than that of the butterfly. The Small White can be seen almost anywhere in the county, with the exception of the highest moors, but it tends to congregate around fields of brassicas. It is, though, more catholic in its choice of larval foodplants, and, unlike the Large White, shows no preference for cultivated species. The butterfly is also highly migratory and migrants add to local populations in the summer.

HABITAT AND ECOLOGY

The Small White enjoys much the same habitats as the Large White, frequenting brassica fields, hedgerows, lanes, rough ground and gardens, wherever there are larval foodplants and plentiful nectar sources; both sexes are attracted by white flowers.

There are two, and in Cornwall certainly three generations a year. The adults usually appear in some numbers during April, although, again in Cornwall, specimens have been seen in March and even in January (Penhallurick 1996), although the latter had probably hibernated as a pupa in a greenhouse. This first brood is generally over by the end of June. The second and later the third broods follow on almost at once and are seen continuously from July onwards to October, during which period numbers are greatly augmented by immigrants; specimens have also been recorded in the county as late as November.

CAUSES OF DECLINE OR INCREASE

Owing to immigration, numbers of this butterfly fluctuate from year to year. There has probably been a slight increase recently, but it is unlikely that the butterfly will ever again reach pest populations. Apart from crop-spraying, it is said that House Sparrows (*Passer domesticus*) and Garden Warblers (*Sylvia borin*) are known to eat the eggs of this species and so exert a measure of natural control (Emmet and Heath 1990). It remains one of the commonest British species.

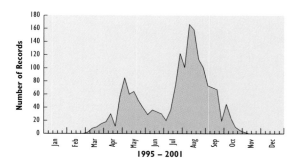

1995 – 2001

CONSERVATION

No conservation of this species is necessary.

LARVAL FOODPLANTS

As well as utilising all cultivated brassicas, it also finds Garlic Mustard (*Alliaria petiolata*), Hedge Mustard (*Sisymbrium officinale*), Charlock (*Sinapis arvensis*) and Wild Cabbage (*Brassica oleracea* var. *oleracea*) equally attractive, in addition to cultivated garden plants such as Nasturtium (*Tropaeolum majus*) and Wallflowers (*Erysimum chieri*); almost any other cruciferous plants will suffice.

ABERRATIONS

Major aberrations are rare, and are mostly associated with the variability of the black markings and the ground colour. A male ab. *immaculata*, where the black markings are absent, was captured at Porthcurno in April 1970 (Russwurm 1978). Ab. *fasciata*, where the two black spots on the forewings of the female are united by a dusting of black scales, was captured west of Portreath in August 1983, while ab. *flava*, a lemon yellow specimen, was seen near St Agnes in July 1955 (Penhallurick 1996).

As with the Large White, the species is seasonally dimorphic, with the summer broods having more extensive black markings, but with a less grey ground colour (Emmet and Heath 1990).

Green-veined White *Pieris napi*

No. of tetrads (1995–2000): 346
Status in Cornwall: resident
Regional priority: none
Regional rate of change: slight decrease, otherwise reasonably stable, +10%

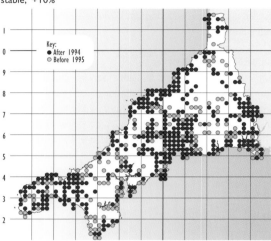

Key:
● After 1994
◦ Before 1995

DISTRIBUTION IN CORNWALL

The species remains widespread and common in Cornwall, despite the drainage of wetlands, since, unlike the other two common Whites, it prefers damper places. Confusion with Large and Small Whites may mean that it is under-represented on the distribution map, which shows less records than for the other Whites.

HABITAT AND ECOLOGY

The Green-veined White can be found on hedges with dense growth, in gardens, damp meadows and alongside lanes and tracks in the county, even on the higher moors. It does not seem to be excessively attracted to cultivated crops; the species is not therefore seen as a pest, although it was reported as having partly destroyed a watercress bed near Bodmin in 1902 (Clark 1906). The butterflies tend to congregate where the foodplants are plentiful, since these also provide a source of early nectar, failing which flowers of bramble and thistle suffice. It is one of Britain's commonest butterflies, and was recorded in 92% of 10km squares during the 1995–99 survey, more than any other butterfly in Britain (Asher *et al.* 2001). Numbers are said to have declined after the droughts of 1975–76 through loss of foodplants, but quickly recovered (Emmet and Heath 1990).

The nominate form does not occur in the British Isles, but there is considerable controversy over the naming of the British subspecies; (Emmet and Heath 1990) provisionally prefer subs. *sabellicae*, which is supposed to be found throughout Britain.

The Green-veined White can be double- or triple- brooded in Cornwall, depending on conditions. It is almost entirely a non-migratory species and the summer broods are seldom augmented by continental specimens, unlike the Large and Small Whites. The first brood emerges in late April or early May, the males appearing several days before the females, although they have been seen in late March in the county. The second brood reaches maturity towards the end of June, although apparently not all then emerge, about half remaining in the pupal state until the next spring. But the butterflies that emerge can, in favourable summers, produce a third generation in late

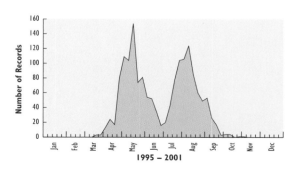

1995 – 2001

August and September, although they have been seen in Cornwall as late as the end of October. The emergences in the following spring come from the surviving pupae of the two or three broods from the previous summer, although by the spring numbers will have been reduced by predators and disease.

Given this breeding pattern, it is possible to see Green-veined Whites in Cornwall throughout the spring, summer and autumn from March to October.

CAUSES OF DECLINE OR INCREASE

There has perhaps been a slight decrease in numbers caused by the draining of wetlands, but this has probably been less important in Cornwall, where agriculture is perhaps not quite so intensive in some places.

CONSERVATION

Maintenance of wetlands and damp meadows, together with Cornish hedges, is essential for this species.

LARVAL FOODPLANTS

Almost any cruciferous plants seem to be attractive, but mostly Lady's Smock (*Cardamine pratensis*), Garlic Mustard (*Alliaria petiolata*), Hedge Mustard (*Sisymbrium officinale*), Watercress (*Rorippa nasturtium-aquaticum*), and Charlock (*Sinapis arvensis*); Hairy Rockcress (*Arabis hirsuta*), which only occurs on calcareous dunes in Cornwall at one or two isolated places on the north coast, can also be used.

ABERRATIONS

A large number are known in the wild, and more extreme forms have been bred in captivity. The lack of recorded aberrations in Cornwall perhaps indicates that not enough attention has been paid to them. The butterfly is seasonally dimorphic as in the Large and Small Whites.

A female ab. *fasciata* was noted near St Austell in July 1994, in which the spots on the forewing are joined to form a black band; it has also been recorded at a much earlier date in the Falmouth area. A female ab. *sulphurea*, a lemon-yellow form, was seen in coition with a normal male at Upton Towans in early September 2000. Dwarf specimens of this species are not uncommon and one was recorded near Lostwithiel in 1989, with another at Par dunes in August 1994.

PIERIDAE

Bath White *Pontia daplicice*

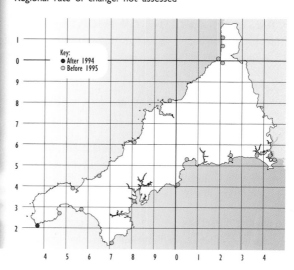

No. of tetrads (1995–2000): 1
Status in Cornwall: rare immigrant
Regional priority: none
Regional rate of change: not assessed

Key:
● After 1994
○ Before 1995

DISTRIBUTION IN CORNWALL

Prior to the great invasion of 1945, this very rare immigrant had only been seen once in the county. It is a common species in the Mediterranean and a well-known migrant in northern France as well as in other parts of northern Europe. In Britain it is an occasional migrant, usually being seen singly, and mainly in the south-east of the country. In 1945, however, Cornwall accounted for over 450 of the 700 or so seen in that year, most of which appeared in the southern counties. The invasion is believed to have arrived on southerly winds, which preceded heavy thunderstorms, and which followed the worst drought in south-western Europe for 150 years (Penhallurick 1996; Smith, F.H.N. 1997).

The first butterflies to arrive in Cornwall in 1945 were seen at Falmouth in mid-July, with others at Mousehole, Carbis Bay, Looe and St Austell at about the same time. Later in the month, few parts of Cornwall had not been visited. Surprisingly, though, there were no reports from west Penwith, but this may have been due to lack of recorders.

Since 1945, they have appeared in the county only singly in five years, with the last record on the south side of Gwennap Head in August 1996.

HABITAT AND ECOLOGY

The adults are highly mobile and can be found in almost any habitat, although it is claimed that Clover (*Trifolium* spp.) and Lucerne (*Medicago sativa*) fields are most favoured (Emmet and Heath 1990). In 1945, they were seen egg-laying in Falmouth Docks, and consequently any rough, unclaimed land with nectar sources will prove satisfactory.

Some confusion may occur between this butterfly and the female Orange-tip (p. 45). Normally the difference in flight periods will prevent this happening, but observers should beware scarce over-wintered Bath Whites flying in April and May and the rare, but noted in Cornwall, second brood female Orange-tip in August and September.

In its homelands, the Bath White has several generations, but it is doubtful if it has ever achieved more than one in Britain. Migrants do not usually arrive before July, and there is evidence of both eggs and larvae being seen later that month near Bude in 1945 (Harbottle 1950), as well as the egg-laying specimens at Falmouth. A number of adults appeared later that year in September and October which may have been the progeny of the earlier arrivals. Specimens appearing in April and May the following year elsewhere in the country imply that some may have successfully over-wintered.

CAUSES OF DECLINE OR INCREASE

As with most immigrants, the frequency of appearance depends entirely on the weather systems of southern Europe.

CONSERVATION

None are necessary for this species.

LARVAL FOODPLANTS

The females, which were observed egg-laying in Falmouth Docks, were doing so on Hedge Mustard (*Sisymbrium officinale*), while the eggs and larvae seen on Bude golf course were on Sea Radish (*Raphanus raphanistrum* ssp. *maritimus*), which is largely confined to the coastal fringes, more especially in the south of Cornwall.

Wild Mignonette (*Reseda lutea*) has also been recorded as a foodplant in Britain, although it is uncommon in Cornwall, but apparently a wide range of crucifers will suffice.

ABERRATIONS

The species is seasonally dimorphic, although the spring generation is rarely seen in Britain. Non-seasonal aberrations are very scarce and none have been recorded in Cornwall.

PIERIDAE

Orange-tip *Anthocharis cardamines*

No. of tetrads (1995–2000): 154
Status in Cornwall: resident
Regional priority: none
Regional rate of change: relatively stable, with fluctuations, +32%

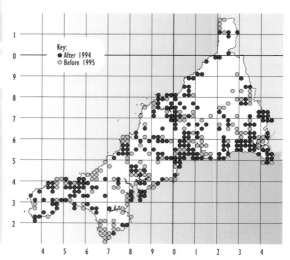

Key:
● After 1994
○ Before 1995

DISTRIBUTION IN CORNWALL

The Orange-tip is widely distributed throughout the county, although perhaps less common in the far west. It is one of the most frequent spring and early-summer butterflies, occurring in almost every 10km square, except for some in north Cornwall; these embrace much of the higher areas of Bodmin Moor, where it has hardly ever been seen, suggesting that it prefers lower-lying ground. Nevertheless there are also some smaller gaps where it has never been recorded, which may be due to the absence of suitable larval foodplants, although so many of these have been identified, that it would be surprising if the female could not find something to her liking almost anywhere.

HABITAT AND ECOLOGY

Both male and female inhabit gardens, hedgerows, damp fields and roadside verges, where they are often found during the flight period fluttering slowly around them, although the female has a more purposeful flight. Both delight in the flowers of Cow Parsley (*Anthriscus sylvestris*), where, at rest with wings closed, they are almost invisible due to the excellent camouflage afforded by the mottled green colouring on the undersides of the hind-wings. But they also enjoy nectaring on garden flowers, among them Aubretia (*Aubretia deltoidea*) and London Pride (*Saxifraga umbrosa × s. spathularis*).

The Orange-tip is normally single-brooded; adults have been seen as early as the beginning of March in Cornwall, although mid-to late April is more normal, with the main flight period occurring from May to June, extending sometimes into July. Specimens have occasionally been recorded in both August and September (Smith, F.N.H. 1997; Penhallurick 1996) and presumably belong to a rare second brood, when the female may be confused with the migrant Bath White.

The male butterfly usually emerges earlier than the female; the latter when first appearing, is inclined to seek shelter in undergrowth, where it is eagerly pursued by the male. After mating the female will take to the wing in search of suitable

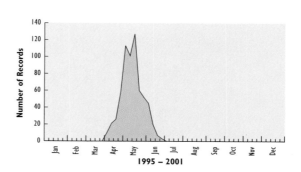

1995 – 2001

foodplants. The female is more frequently observed later in the season than the male, when it can be confused with other Whites, unless seen at rest. Neither male nor female are ever seen in great numbers in one place, and the species is something of a wanderer, not forming tight colonies.

CAUSES OF DECLINE OR INCREASE

The Orange-tip is subject to periodic declines in populations, such as happened in west Cornwall in the early 1990s. This may be due to an increased incidence of Tachinid Fly (*Phryxe vulgaris*) which feeds on the caterpillars (Thomas and Lewington 1991), and which appears to be mainly confined to the coastal regions in Cornwall, or to cannibalism among young larvae. A period of bad weather during the egg-laying season may also cause the female to be less careful in her choice of plants, resulting in poor numbers of caterpillars. Yet, after a decrease, it seems to be able to re-establish itself with ease, given the right conditions, and is now comparatively common again in the west of the county.

Female Orange-tip.

CONSERVATION

Undoubtedly the cutting and spraying of roadside verges, which can kill the insects in all stages of development, will affect populations. Happily in Cornwall spraying of verges with herbicides has virtually ceased. Since responsibility for roadside cutting has recently been transferred, except on major roads, from the County Council to individual landowners, this activity has also been delayed until July or even later, while some minor roads and small lanes remain uncut throughout the year.

Distribution maps, decade by decade since 1960, show a distinct increase in populations, but they fail to pick out the decline in the early 1990s. Consequently one is left with the uncomfortable feeling that the increase is due to more observers now in the field than to actual butterflies.

LARVAL FOODPLANTS

Over 30 foodplants have been listed (Penhallurick 1996) but the most favoured seem to be Lady's Smock (*Cardamines pratensis*), Garlic Mustard (*Alliaria petiolata*) and Hedge Mustard (*Sisymbrium officinale*). Garlic Mustard is less common on the granites of west Cornwall, where its place is taken by Hedge Mustard.

ABERRATIONS

Although they are not uncommon in the Orange-tip, few have been recorded from the county. Several of the diminutive form, where also the central black spot on the forewing of the male is instead located on the edge of the orange patch (ab. *turritis* = ab. *hesperidis*) were seen in the Penzance area at the end of the century before last. A diminutive male, about half normal size, but with the usual markings, was recorded in 1998 near Hayle. A male (ab. *crassipuncta*), where the black discoidal spot on the forewing is much enlarged, was seen at Luxulyan in 1994. The latter form is usually restricted to the female.

Green Hairstreak *Callophrys rubi*

LYCAENIDAE

No. of tetrads (1995–2000): 39
Status in Cornwall: resident
Regional priority: none
Regional rate of change: stable and increasing, +30%

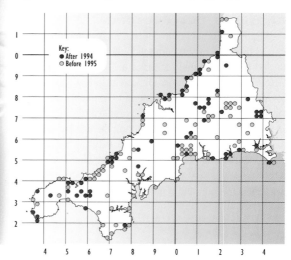

Key:
● After 1994
○ Before 1995

DISTRIBUTION IN CORNWALL

The Green Hairstreak is an elusive butterfly and is probably one of the most under-recorded species in Cornwall. Nevertheless it is widespread and at one time or another has been recorded in most of the 10km squares, if not in all tetrads. It is sometimes argued that it is commoner on the coast, particularly on the north coast, but recent records do not fully support this contention, although there is a curious gap in mid-Cornwall. Even in its known colonies, numbers are seldom large, and in 1997, the maximum number seen was five; more normally, they are seen in ones or twos. This being so, some years pass without any records for a particular site. For instance in 1994–97 it was recorded at three separate sites on the coastal footpaths at Carbis Bay, but none were seen in 1998–99. It was recorded in 1998 at Upton Towans, near the old explosive works, but in no other year, except for a possible sighting at Gwithian Towans in 1999; similarly it has been seen at Trencom Hill only in 1997, and in a clearing in Godolphin Woods in 1998.

HABITAT AND ECOLOGY

The butterfly inhabits unimproved land where there is usually some scrub cover, such as blackthorn, gorse and broom, willow, holly and hawthorn; the male likes to fly around the tops of these bushes, but, when at rest, is almost invisible due to the green colouring of the underside of its wings. Consequently it is most likely to be seen in coastal, and in inland river, valleys where the steepness of the ground has kept agriculture at bay, or in woodland rides, old railway lines and footpaths and bridleways.

The Green Hairstreak is mainly to be seen in May and June, although in Cornwall specimens have been recorded as early as the beginning of April and as late as the end of July (Penhallurick 1996). There is only one brood.

CAUSES OF DECLINE OR INCREASE

It is very difficult to estimate whether or not this species has suffered a decline in Cornwall. Nationally, destruction of habitat has caused the Green Hairstreak to be less common than

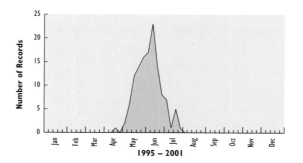

1995 – 2001

formerly (Asher *et al.* 2001) although the Cornish populations may not have been so much affected (Penhallurick 1996), since most of its known habitats are unsuitable for agriculture.

CONSERVATION

Maintenance of habitat is the foremost consideration. The most serious threat is probably destruction caused by development for houses, caravan sites or industry, but uncontrolled clearance of scrub in so-called 'tidying-up' operations at old mine sites or along footpaths and bridleways should be carefully watched.

LARVAL FOODPLANTS

Green Hairstreak caterpillars feed on a variety of foodplants, among which Penhallurick (1996) quotes Gorse (*Ulex* sp.), Bird's-foot Trefoil (*Lotus corniculatus*), Bramble (*Rubus* sp.), Ling (*Calluna vulgaris*) and related species, Dyer's Greenweed (*Genista tinctoria*) and Petty Whin (*Genista anglica*), which is largely restricted to the Lizard. Emmet and Heath (1990, 121) added Broom (*Cytisus scoparius*), Bilberry (*Vaccinium myrtillus*) and Dogwood (*Cornus sanguinea*), which is restricted to south-east Cornwall.

ABERRATIONS

There are a number of aberrations, mostly related to the appearance of the white spots on the underside of the wings. So far, however, no aberrations have been reported from Cornwall.

Brown Hairstreak *Thecla betulae*

LYCAENIDAE

No. of tetrads (1995–2000): 0
Status in Cornwall: doubtful resident
Regional priority: high
Regional rate of change: increasing, +23%

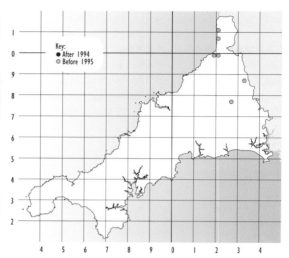

Key:
● After 1994
◉ Before 1995

DISTRIBUTION IN CORNWALL

As with many Hairstreaks, the Brown Hairstreak is a rarely-seen butterfly, inhabiting the tops of trees, and seldom coming to ground level; observers have sat for hours, in excellent weather, and in known colonies, without seeing a single specimen. Consequently, although it is still resident in Devon, it has not often been seen recently in Cornwall, where it is now a doubtful breeding species. If it does survive, then it is most probably in the woodland areas of north and east Cornwall. The last evidence of the butterfly breeding in the county was in the winter of 1988–89, when five eggs were found on blackthorn at Werrington, north of Launceston, but these may have been the product of a wandering female from over the nearby border with Devon. Although there are records of the butterfly in north-east Cornwall at Poundstock and Morwenstow in the post-1960s, these have now been considered as doubtful and relegated to pre-1940 (Heath *et al.* 1984). There was also an unauthenticated record from Tehidy Woods in 1942, which would have represented the only appearance of the butterfly in west Cornwall.

But given the butterfly's shy and secretive habits, it would be surprising if it did not perhaps linger on, in some out-of-the-way corners of the Lynher and Tamar valleys, close to its stronghold in Devon.

HABITAT AND ECOLOGY

The Brown Hairstreak is a woodland butterfly, normally flying around the tops of oak and ash trees, where it nectars on the honeydew provided by aphids; it prefers trees on woodland edges and usually adopts a master tree where males and females congregate to seek mates. Very occasionally the butterflies come down to ground level in order to nectar on, for example, brambles and hemp agrimony, while mated females distribute themselves among hedges of blackthorn for egg-laying.

In the final stages of larval development in captivity, they become moderately attractive to ants, although no examples of this behaviour have been recorded in the wild. But the pupae become highly attractive and they are often buried in cells of loose earth by *Lasius niger*.

CAUSES OF DECLINE OR INCREASE

The chief causes of decline have been the removal of hedges, and the annual trimming of the survivors, which now takes place too frequently; 50–100% of eggs laid on a hedge can be destroyed by injudicious flailing (Emmet and Heath 1996), especially since the preferred egg-laying site is on the recent growth and therefore on the more vulnerable outsides of the hedge. Moreover the larvae can be subject to heavy predation by invertebrates and by insectivorous birds (Bourn and Warren 1998).

CONSERVATION

The most worthwhile contributions to conservation would be to persuade highway authorities, farmers and landowners to discontinue annual trimming of blackthorn hedges in areas where colonies might be present.

LARVAL FOODPLANTS

One-or two-year old growth of Blackthorn (*Prunus spinosa*) is normally used, but other *Prunus* species, such as Bullace (*Prunus domestica* ssp. *insititia*) has occasionally been employed, although the latter has a restricted distribution in Cornwall (French *et al.* 1999).

ABERRATIONS

Aberrations are rare in this species and none have been recorded in Cornwall.

LYCAENIDAE

Purple Hairstreak *Neozephyrus (Quercusia) quercus*

No. of tetrads (1995–2000): 75
Status in Cornwall: resident
Regional priority: low
Regional rate of change: increasing, +15%

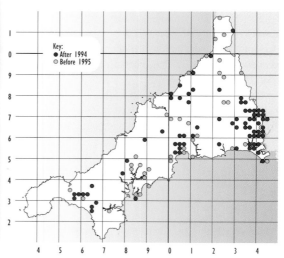

Key:
● After 1994
◐ Before 1995

DISTRIBUTION IN CORNWALL

The Purple Hairstreak is locally common throughout all Cornwall and has been recorded in almost every 10km square except for those in the Land's End peninsula, where lack of larval foodplant militates against it; for that reason it is also scarce in the Lizard away from the Helford river oakwoods. However the adult is probably under-recorded, as with most Hairstreaks, and other butterflies, which prefer flying around the tops of trees. Most recent records of the butterfly have been in central and eastern parts of the county; surveys over the last five years have revealed only four new sites in the west, and none of them in the far west.

One of the certain places to see the butterfly is on a fine day in the woodland of the Godolphin Estate, newly acquired by the National Trust. Due to the low elevation of many of the oaks here, observations can often be made at close quarters. In July 1997 over 90 specimens were seen flying simultaneously around a single tree. But as with many other species, the butterfly is subject to annual fluctuations, for the following year only a few adults were seen on the same tree, even though it was visited on a number of occasions.

Probably the best time of day to see a Purple Hairstreak is on a warm, still summer evening in mid-July when they tend to congregate at a low level, with their wings open, basking in the last rays of the sun.

HABITAT AND ECOLOGY

The butterfly primarily inhabits woodlands, providing they contain oaks, which is the larval foodplant. But they can also be found on isolated trees, such as one growing in a hedge, which is quite sufficient to support a colony. As well as oaks, the adults can frequent other trees such as Beech (*Fagus sylvaticus*) and more particularly Ash (*Fraxinus excelsior*) where they enjoy feeding on the honeydew provided by aphids. Likewise they have been seen clustering around a small Alder Buckthorn bush (*Frangula alnus*), situated among oaks at Godolphin, and nectaring on the flowers; they also nectar on bramble flowers (*Rubus* spp.).

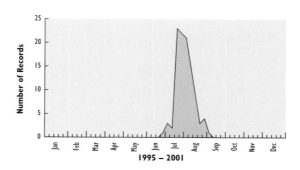

1995 – 2001

At some stage in the larval development, ants are involved, and pupae have been found in ants' nests; both *Myrmica scabrinodis* and *Myrmica ruginodis* are known to be suitable hosts, both of which are common and widespread in Cornwall.

The adult butterfly is normally on the wing through July and August, with a peak in the middle of this period; they have though been recorded in late June, and until the middle of September in Cornwall.

CAUSES OF DECLINE OR INCREASE

The Purple Hairstreak seems to be holding its own in Cornwall despite changes in woodland management, and there are even signs of an increase.

Loss of oak trees and fragmentation of wooded landscapes are the chief threats, although the latter is perhaps not quite so serious, given the butterfly's habit of colonising individual trees (Spalding with Bourn 2000).

CONSERVATION

Woods should be furnished with oaks of varying ages where possible, so as to give an undulating canopy, and with sufficient clearings to maintain warm, sunny lower branches.

LARVAL FOODPLANTS

Any species of Oak (*Quercus* spp.) appears to suffice for the larvae, although it is said (Penhallurick 1996) that the Turkey Oak (*Quercus cerris*) is less favoured in Cornwall. They have even been found on the Evergreen Oak (*Quercus ilex*), although there are no records of this from the county (Asher *et al.* 2001).

ABERRATIONS

Aberrations are uncommon in this butterfly and are mainly concerned with variations in the purple colouration of the upper surface of the wings. None have been recorded in Cornwall.

White-letter Hairstreak *Satyrium w-album*

LYCAENIDAE

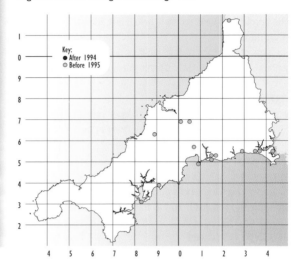

No. of tetrads (1995–2000): 0
Status in Cornwall: probably extinct, but may still be resident
Regional priority: medium
Regional rate of change: decreasing, +1%

Key:
● After 1994
○ Before 1995

DISTRIBUTION IN CORNWALL

Frohawk (1934) recorded that the White-letter Hairstreak was seemingly absent from Cornwall and the first specimen was not authenticated until 1945 at Pendennis. After its brief residence in the county, it has apparently disappeared again, the last firm record being at Pontsmill, Lanlivery in 1985. But it has always been a scarce species in the county, being confined to three or four colonies on the south coast east of Falmouth, and to a couple of colonies on the north coast, with one inland near Bodmin; the latter are almost certainly extinct (Penhallurick 1996, Smith, F.H.N. 1997), since no adults have been seen since the 1970s. It is an elusive butterfly, flying mainly round tree tops, which does not make positive identification easy, even when seen.

Nevertheless, colonies may still survive in secluded and out-of-the-way places, and it is always worth looking. In 1994, a butterfly resembling the size, colour and flight of a White-letter Hairstreak was seen on two separate occasions, near Hayle, flying around the tops of low trees and not far distant from scrub elm. Unfortunately it could not be confirmed; the colony, if there was one, was never located and no butterflies have been seen since.

HABITAT AND ECOLOGY

The White-letter Hairstreak's elusive habits have already been referred to. It is mostly seen flying high up around the canopies of the larval foodplant, and other trees, where aphids produce honeydew; it seldom descends to ground level, but it is occasionally attracted to privet and bramble blossoms and has also been noted nectaring on Hemp Agrimony (*Eupatorium cannabinum*).

The butterfly is on the wing generally from early July to mid-August, although specimens have been seen in Cornwall in late June.

CAUSES OF DECLINE OR INCREASE

The decline in Cornwall has been due to: 1) the original scarcity of English Elm (*Ulmus procera*) and Wych Elm (*Ulmus glabra*) and 2) to the spread of Dutch Elm Disease, which has killed many of the trees on which the larvae may have fed, and the subsequent destruction of the regrowth in scrubland and hedgerow.

CONSERVATION

The White-letter Hairstreak may be encouraged to return to Cornwall by the planting of disease-resistant varieties of Elm (Spalding with Bourn 2000).

LARVAL FOODPLANTS

Tradition stated that the butterfly only bred on mature, flowering elm species, of which the Wych Elm (*Ulmus glabra*), English Elm (*Ulmus procera*) and the Small-leaved Elm (*Ulmus minor*) were the most favoured. Since the destruction of so many elm trees by Dutch Elm Disease, this Hairstreak appears to have adapted to the new conditions and will utilise the suckers produced from the roots of dead trees, and on younger elm growth in hedges and copses. The butterfly never appears to have had a liking for Cornish Elm (*Ulmus minor* ssp. *angustifolia*), or for its hybrids with other species. This would presumably account for the butterfly's original scarcity in Cornwall, since the English Elm was rare and the Wych Elm widely scattered.

ABERRATIONS

Aberrations are uncommon in this species, and none have been recorded in Cornwall.

LYCAENIDAE

Small Copper *Lycaena phlaeas*

No. of tetrads (1995–2000): 281
Status in Cornwall: resident
Regional priority: none
Regional rate of change: increasing, +14%

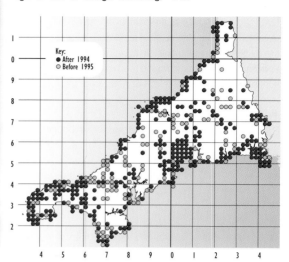

Key:
● After 1994
○ Before 1995

DISTRIBUTION IN CORNWALL

This small butterfly is probably one of the most widespread in Cornwall, occurring on all except the highest ground. The species, though, shows a preference for rough, open areas, either flat or undulating, hill slopes or coastal dunes. It can also be found in woodland clearings, on roadside verges and railway embankments, and even in gardens.

HABITAT AND ECOLOGY

The adults seek out sheltered, wind-free, dry and warm corners in any of the areas mentioned above. There they will bask on a stone, bare ground or on low-growing flowers and vegetation. They tend to form small colonies, where ample larval foodplants exist, although the mobility of the butterfly means that it can often be seen almost anywhere.

The nominate form does not occur in Britain, where, in the south of the country, the subsp. *eleus* takes its place (Emmet and Heath 1990).

With its relatively short life-cycle it usually produces four broods in Cornwall, and perhaps a fifth occurs in very favourable summers, providing drought has not withered the foodplants. Consequently it can be seen in the county in almost any month from mid-March to late November, the later broods apparently overlapping. But in general adults do not appear in numbers until mid-April, and there is usually a gap in mid-June when none are about. Numbers are usually at their peak in July and August.

CAUSES OF DECLINE OR INCREASE

Populations fluctuate according to the weather. Cool, wet summers cause colonies in shadier, woodland areas to slump, while hot, dry summers affect the larval foodplants, with a subsequent decline in later broods.

CONSERVATION

No conservation of this species is necessary, but it might be worthwhile to consider a management agreement for one of

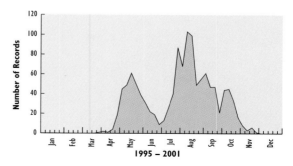

1995 – 2001

the larger colonies, such as Carloggas Downs, where sorrels grow adjacent to abundant heathers for nectaring, on a south-facing slope; the site produces perhaps 500+ Small Coppers in a favourable season through its four generations.

LARVAL FOODPLANTS

Either Common Sorrel (*Rumex acetosa*) or Sheep's Sorrel (*Rumex acetosella*) can be used, both of which are common in Cornwall. Broad-leaved Dock (*Rumex obtusifolius*) is said to be used occasionally, but is not thought to make a great contribution. The first-brood Small Coppers tend to lay their eggs on large, mature plants of Sorrel, while later in the season small young plants are selected.

ABERRATIONS

There are many named aberrations of this species, of which a number have been recorded in Cornwall. There is considerable variation in the black spotting on the forewings, in the alteration of the copper colouration on the forewings as well as the copper band on the hindwings. A comparatively common form has a row of blue spots inside the copper band of the latter (ab. *caeruleopunctata*) and has been seen at a number of sites in the county; in 1994 there were over a dozen reports. Others were seen in 1960 at Newlyn East and at Pentewan in 1994. The black or nearly-black form ab. *fuscae* was observed at Bude in 1976, also at Penberthy in 1996 and near Hayle in 1998. Ab. *cuprinus*, where the coppery colour is replaced by gold or creamy-white was seen at Bude in 1976, with a creamy-white specimen at Upton Towans in 1993. The silvery-white ab. *schmidtii* was recorded in 1994 at Otterham, near Boscastle, near Looe in the 1970s, two near Delabole in 1987, and at Par dunes in the mid-1990s. Four specimens of ab. *obsoleta*, where the copper band on the hindwing is absent, or nearly so, were recorded at St Agnes in 1955–56 and one at Bude in 1976. Where only part of the band is absent in ab. *semi-obsoleta*, specimens were noted at Pentewan in 1994, and at Penhale in the mid-1990s. A dwarf specimen of ab. *radiata*, where streaks of copper colour run up the veins of the hindwings, was noted at Gwithian in 1955; normal-sized *radiata* have been recorded in west Cornwall in 1913, at Trevissick Farm in 1955 and at Zelah in 1959. An unnamed aberration, where four large bold markings appeared on the upper surface of the hindwings was observed at Breney Common in 2000.

Small Copper, ab. *caeruleopunctata* (top) and ab. *schmidtii* (bottom).

Long-tailed Blue *Lampides boeticus*

LYCAENIDAE

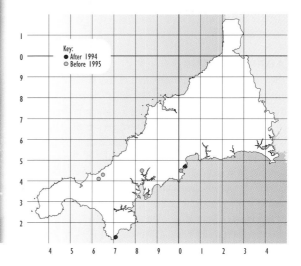

No. of tetrads (1995–2000): 2
Status in Cornwall: rare and infrequent immigrant
Regional priority: none
Regional rate of change: variable

Key:
● After 1994
◐ Before 1995

DISTRIBUTION IN CORNWALL

The species is a rare migrant to Cornwall from southern Europe. Until the year 2001, there had only been five accepted records (Smith, F.H.N. 1997): in 1904 near Truro, in 1940 near Treswithian, two in 1945 at St Mawes, and one in 1967 at Polstreath. In 2001 there were two more positive sightings at Pentewan and the Lizard, with rumours of a third individual. Doubtless other specimens of this unobtrusive butterfly have been overlooked.

HABITAT AND ECOLOGY

The butterfly is often found in flower-rich areas, particularly gardens, where there may be larval foodplants, or on open downland. Its rapid and jerky flight makes confirmation of the species difficult.

It is most likely to be seen in late July to a 'peak' in September, declining through October, although November records are not unknown. Breeding in Britain is unproved, but not impossible, since it is multi-brooded in its native habitats; nine specimens caught in one garden in Kent in September 1926, suggest that local breeding had occurred. Eggs have also been located in Surrey, and larva have been seen in Sussex (Emmet and Heath 1990).

CAUSES OF DECLINE OR INCREASE

The presence of the butterfly in Cornwall tends to coincide with years which are good for other immigrants, such as 1945; but this need not be so, as in 2001, which was not noted for other migrant species.

CONSERVATION

Little can be done apart from planting larval foodplants along the south coast.

LARVAL FOODPLANTS

Various leguminous plants can be used, among them the Broad-leaved Everlasting Pea (*Lathyrus latifolius*) and Broom (*Cytisus scoparius*); the larvae feed on the flowers or seed pods. Probably the garden Sweet Pea (*Lathyrus odoratus*) would suffice, while senna pods used as an indoor decoration have been known to be used.

Small Blue *Cupido minimus*

No. of tetrads (1995–2000): 0
Status in Cornwall: doubtful resident
Regional priority: medium
Regional rate of change: increasing, +31%

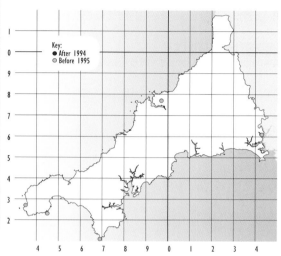

Key:
● After 1994
◯ Before 1995

DISTRIBUTION IN CORNWALL

The status of the Small Blue in Cornwall is uncertain. Early in the last century specimens were taken near Saltash, two of which proved to have been wrongly identified. More recently a male was seen at Landulph in 1988 and another was captured near the Rock dunes, St Minver, in 1991. The former may have been a stray from a colony over the Devon border where one was known in the 1980s in an old railway cutting, long since destroyed, in Plymouth; the latter may represent a small and hitherto unknown colony (Smith, F.H.N. 1997). But, although Rock dunes appear to contain abundant suitable habitats for the Small Blue, with many small sheltered hollows, ample larval foodplants and Wild Privet (*Ligustrum vulgare*) as nectar sources, no other evidence for the butterfly has been found there. There have also been unauthenticated records from Polzeath in 1954, Padstow in 1970 and the Lizard in 1976.

Attempts have been made to introduce this butterfly to west Cornwall, at the Lizard in 1982–83, Land's End and Lamorna in 1983–84, without success, none surviving even in the following years (Morton 1985); the three relevant sites are shown on the distribution map.

HABITAT AND ECOLOGY

The Small Blue is a somewhat sedentary species which inhabits calcareous grassland, sand dunes and areas associated with them, such as abandoned quarries and old railway cuttings, so long as they are reasonably sheltered, dry and with areas of short or sparse vegetation.

The butterfly forms small, discrete colonies, and individuals rarely travel more than about 50m from them, although in hot summers vagrants have been found up to 17km away (Asher *et al.* 2001).

The adults generally emerge from late May until early July, and there is a small, partial second generation in late July into August.

CAUSES OF DECLINE OR INCREASE

The chief cause of decline is the destruction of habitat, either by lack of grazing to form the necessary short vegetation followed by scrub encroachment or by overgrazing, which destroys the foodplants.

CONSERVATION

There is little that can be done by way of conservation for this species in Cornwall, so long as the localities of possible colonies remain unknown.

LARVAL FOODPLANTS

The only foodplant known is Kidney Vetch (*Anthyllis vulneraria*), and the larvae live almost exclusively on the developing flower heads. This is a common coastal plant in Cornwall, but its flowering periods may not suit the Small Blue, especially in the west.

ABERRATIONS

A number of aberrations of this species have been recognised but none have been recorded in Cornwall.

Short-tailed Blue *Cupido (Everes) argiades*

No. of tetrads (1995–2000): 0
Status in Cornwall: very rare migrant
Regional priority: none
Regional rate of change: not assessed

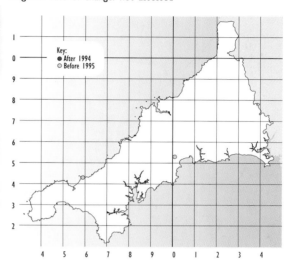

Key:
● After 1994
○ Before 1995

DISTRIBUTION IN CORNWALL

Only three specimens of this very rare immigrant have so far been recorded in Cornwall; two of them were seen in the great migration year of 1945, when one was captured in Falmouth and another was seen at St Austell. The third appeared at Godrevy in 1952.

It is common on the heaths of Brittany, from where the Cornish specimens may have originated, although it shows no obvious migratory habits, and is not a strong flier.

HABITAT AND ECOLOGY

There is no evidence that this butterfly has bred in Britain. It can be found on scrubby grasslands and heaths and also on woodland fringes and in clearings.

In Europe there are two broods, which coincide with those of the Silver-studded Blue (p. 60) and with which in appearance it could be confused, flying from May to June, and July to September. Confusion could also arise with the Small Blue (p. 57), although the rarity of the latter in Cornwall, makes this unlikely.

CAUSES OF DECLINE OR INCREASE; CONSERVATION

No conservation is necessary for this species; neither is it possible to estimate rates of decline or increase.

LARVAL FOODPLANTS

Mostly leguminous plants are used of which many are common in Cornwall, such as Common Bird's-foot Trefoil (*Lotus corniculatus*), Red Clover (*Trifolium pratense*) and Tufted Vetch (*Vicia cracca*); European Gorse (*Ulex europaeus*) is also quoted (Asher *et al*. 2001).

ABERRATIONS

No aberrations have been recorded among the British specimens.

Silver-studded Blue *Plebeius (Plebejus) argus*

No. of tetrads (1995–2000): 35
Status in Cornwall: resident
Regional priority: high
Regional rate of change: decreasing, -12%

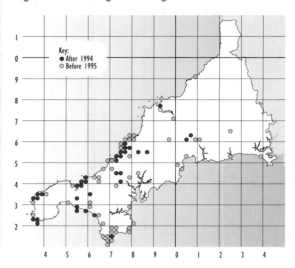

Key:
● After 1994
○ Before 1995

DISTRIBUTION IN CORNWALL

The Silver-studded Blue has nearly always been restricted to the western half of the county, although before 1995 it had been recorded near Boscastle and Liskeard. In the west it is largely confined to the coastal regions, and some of the strongest colonies are found on the dunes at Penhale Sands, from where it spreads as far as St Agnes, at Godrevy, and at Phillack, Gwithian and Upton Towans; surprisingly there is only one very weak colony on Lelant Towans, which may not survive, since clearly the Hayle estuary forms a barrier, across which reinforcing adults cannot travel. It is also to be found in strength in a succession of colonies on the stretch of coast running northwards from Botallack to Pendeen Watch, with another group of colonies north of Gwennap Head. It has been reported as well on the coastal footpath at Kelynack and Cape Cornwall. On the south coast, there is a large colony east of Cudden Point, but colonies at Rinsey Cove and Trewavas Head are small and weak, and no butterflies have been seen there since 1996. Colonies have also been reported on the dunes between Porthleven and Loe Bar and, in the Lizard peninsula, at Kynance and Ruan Minor.

Inland, a small colony was found at Penberthy in 1996–97, in the area of the old mines, although no adults were recorded in 1998–99. Similarly, a single sighting on Binner Downs in 1995 has not been repeated, and the existence of a colony there must remain in doubt. The strongest inland colonies are at Wheal Maid, on United Downs near Truro, and Breney Common. Smaller colonies exist at Wheal Busy, Chacewater, at Penhallow on Newlyn Downs and at Tregoss Moor.

But perhaps the most encouraging record of any for this butterfly is that at Allen's Shaft, and its extension into the Bunny, at Botallack. Attempts were made in the early 1980s to re-open this shaft as part of Geevor Mines and much disturbance of the surrounding surface took place, while a good deal of waste was tipped in the Bunny. But by 1991 all mining had ceased at Geevor; Allen's Shaft had never been fully re-opened, and the site now quickly reverted to nature. Yet by 1996, when the site was first revisited, a strong colony of Silver-studded Blues had re-established itself, not only on the disturbed ground around the shaft but also extending into the Bunny.

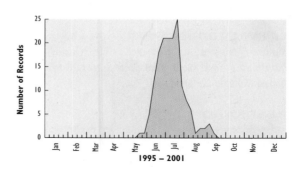

1995 – 2001

HABITAT AND ECOLOGY

The caterpillar is attended by ants, and both *Lasius niger* and *L. alienus* have been recorded (Thomas, C.D. 1983). *L. niger* is the associated species at Wheal Maid and Wheal Busy; *L. alienus* takes its place at Penhale Dunes and Upton Towans. At other sites the association is less clear. Pupation usually occurs in holes in the ground, into which the ants will move, often constructing nests around the chrysalis, and Mendel and Parsons (1987) showed that this process occurs more often than the alternative of caterpillars being carried into ants' nests to pupate. Nevertheless a single larva was observed moving into the nest of *L. alienus* on Gear Sands in 1998. The habit might account for the poor showing of adult butterflies in 1998, when June was a month of successive torrential rainstorms; many ants' nests would have been flooded, possibly drowning the pupae, particularly on sites away from the well-drained dunes.

Two types of habitat occur in Cornwall for this butterfly: dunes and heaths. The dunes support a typical calcareous flora with areas of short turf, cropped by rabbits, interspersed with patches of longer grasses and scrub; most larvae appear to occur within large areas of bare sand or earth, which heats up rapidly in the sun. In contrast the adults seem to prefer the long grasses, providing the stems are sparsely distributed and not over about 0.75m high, and they obviously provide shelter, and resting and roosting places. A mixture of heathers, dwarf gorse, vetches, other plants and grasses is chosen on heathland, rather than undiluted heather, although the colony at Wheal Maid depends almost entirely on heather. Many of these sites are characterised by large areas of bare ground, sometimes metal-contaminated; the site at Breney Common on the other hand is well-covered in vegetation. Dense bracken or scrub seems to form insurmountable barriers. The colonies are usually but not always, to be found on warm, south-facing (east round south to west) slopes, or in areas otherwise protected from strong winds, such as the bunkers of the old explosive works on Upton Towans.

The butterfly lives in close-knit colonies of varying size and was originally thought not to wander more than about 50m from them (Thomas and Lewington 1991). More recently though, this view has been modified and in some cases a small proportion of adults have been observed up to 1.5km from their colonies; the maximum distance recorded is 4km (Asher *et al.* 2001). This revised view has been supported by recent observations in Cornwall, where at Upton and Gwithian Towans, and at the group of colonies north of Botallack, movement between colonies has been recorded with some frequency in every year between 1997 and 2000.

A courtship was witnessed at Wheal Cock on 2 August 1996. It started with the usual rapid fluttering of wings by both male and female. The latter, still fluttering, then perched on top of heather, while the former continued his dance around her. They gradually descended into the base of the heather plant, but every 3–4 minutes the male would re-emerge to regain fresh energy by basking in the sun and taking sips of heather nectar. During his absence, the female now remained quiet and motionless, but with half-open wings, awaiting his return. Refreshed, he would once more descend into the undergrowth and the fluttering would begin again until, after 34 minutes, coition was finally achieved.

The Silver-studded Blue appears earlier on the dunes of Cornwall than on the corresponding heaths, and the end of May has been reported at Perran Sands. More normally it appears in the first week of June on the dunes (3 June 2002 at Upton Towans) whereas it was the middle of July 1999 before any numbers were seen at Wheal Cock, although late June has been recorded at Goss Moor. This first brood on the dunes is usually finished by mid-August at the latest.

It is usually claimed that the Silver-studded Blue produces only one brood of adult butterflies in Britain. Detailed observations at Upton Towans over the last six years have shown that the Silver-studded Blue is capable of producing a definite, partial second brood, with a distinct gap between it and the first brood (Wacher 2002). It thus follows southern European examples, which commonly produce a second brood, and many other Blues in Britain. The flight period of this second brood in Cornwall begins in the last ten days of August and seldom lasts beyond the first week in September. Penhallurick (1996) records very late specimens at Rock, Porthgwarra and St Keverne, but these are unlikely to form part of a definite second generation as undoubtedly occurs at Upton. The colonies at Rock and St Keverne are now probably extinct. Nevertheless his records of late specimens at Upton confirm the subsequent findings there.

CAUSES OF DECLINE OR INCREASE

Although it continues to hold its own in a number of places, there can be no doubt that there has been a decline since 1995 even in west Cornwall, especially in the Lizard and on the north coast between Godrevy and St Agnes. Deterioration of habitat is probably the main cause, with the encroachment of bracken and scrub, the dominance of over-mature heathland, the loss of bare ground and a decrease in habitat structural diversity. Poor weather in June is another factor and may have resulted in 1998 in the extinction of the weak colonies at Penberthy, Rinsey Cove and Trewavas Head.

CONSERVATION

The maintenance of suitable habitats is of prime importance, particularly in, and around, the neighbourhood of existing colonies; appropriate authorities should be made aware of the requirements (Ravenscroft and Warren 1996). Re-introduction is probably not the answer to the decline.

LARVAL FOODPLANTS

Emmet and Heath (1990) quote 12 species of foodplant, among which are Gorses (*Ulex* spp.), Heaths (*Erica* spp.), Ling (*Calluna vulgaris*) on heathland, and Rock-roses (*Helianthemum* spp.) and Bird's-foot Trefoil (*Lotus corniculatus*) on calcareous soils; Rock-roses are absent from Cornwall, and it should also be noted that Gorse grows on dunes, while Bird's-foot Trefoil can occur on mixed heathland. Broom (*Cytisus scoparius*), Petty Whin (*Genista anglica*), Restharrow (*Ononis repens*) and other leguminous plants have also been recorded. In Cornwall the main foodplants are heathers on heathland areas and Bird's-foot Trefoil on sand dunes. It is interesting to note that on the heathland site at Wheal Busy, the foodplant is Bird's-foot Trefoil and it is possible to speculate that this colony arrived with sand taken from the coastal dunes to be loaded onto trucks on the adjacent railway.

Two females were observed egg-laying at Cudden Point, in 1999; one chose a new shoot of Ling (*Calluna vulgaris*) and the other the dead flowerhead of Kidney Vetch (*Anthyllis vulneraria*).

ABERRATIONS

Many aberrations are known for this species, but few have so far been recorded in Cornwall. Five gynandromorphs were reported from Gwithian Towans in 1955–56, where also it is said that the blue form of the female occurs. One of the latter was indeed seen at Upton Towans in July 2000, and appeared indistinguishable from illustrations of the extinct *masseyi* form, which used to inhabit Westmorland. In 1954, a female ab. *privata* or ab. *caeca*, where the underside spots are reduced or absent, was similarly recorded at Gwithian Towans. A now-extinct colony at Park Shady near St Agnes produced, in 1955, both a male and a female ab. *fuscenscens*, where the orange lunules are replaced by dark brown. A female, similar to ab. *juncta*, with bold black markings inside the orange lunules on the underside of both hindwings, was recorded at Penhale Sands in June 1993.

Silver-studded Blue, ab.

Brown Argus *Aricia agestis*

No. of tetrads (1995–2000): 23
Status in Cornwall: resident
Regional priority: low
Regional rate of change: increasing, +39%

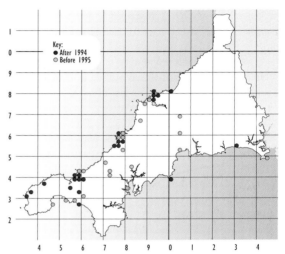

Key:
● After 1994
○ Before 1995

DISTRIBUTION IN CORNWALL

The Brown Argus is mainly confined to the dunes of north-west Cornwall, but it appears to be extending its range throughout the west of the county. Its three main strongholds, though, remain the dunes around Rock and Padstow, Gear and Penhale Sands, and Upton and Gwithian Towans. Sightings of the butterfly have never been frequent in the east, although specimens were seen near Rame in 1979 and near Looe in 1987. In 1994 it was recorded at Dodman Point. In Penwith it now appears at a number of both coastal and inland sites: Rinsey Cove between 1996–98, Cudden Point in 1999, Gwennap Head in 1997, Wheal Cock near Botallack in 1999 and Pendeen Watch in 1997; inland it has been seen near Angarrack in 1997 and near Truthwall in the same year. But the most surprising of all was a specimen that arrived in the green lane beside a house near Connor Downs in 1996, to be followed by a female and two males in the garden some days later; specimens again visited the garden later that year and in 1997. A search of the neighbourhood in 1997 revealed the parent colony at Gwinear Road disused railway station; they were seen again there in 1998.

HABITAT AND ECOLOGY

The adult butterflies inhabit small, loose-knit colonies, usually containing very few individuals, in areas where the turf is kept short by rabbits or other means and where larval foodplants grow in abundance, such as on the calcareous dunes. Elsewhere, on more neutral or acid soils, it can cope with taller vegetation, so long as it is fairly sparse. Despite its colonial habits, the butterfly is obviously capable of flying some distance, and is more mobile than some other Blues; the early 1990s saw a considerable expansion of its range in Britain, which was reflected in Cornwall (Asher *et al.* 2001). It has now adapted to a wider range of habitats, which include road verges and non-rotational set-aside fields. There is evidence that the increases are related to good summer temperatures between June and August, while wet, cool summers have a negative effect.

There are normally two broods: the first mainly in May and June, although specimens have been seen in late April in

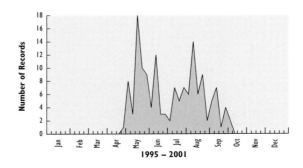

Number of Records

1995 – 2001

Cornwall; the second in July and August or early September. Emmet and Heath (1990) refer to a small third generation in southern Europe, so it is not impossible that some very late emergences, quoted by Penhallurick (1996) in late September, belong to a partial third brood. Several butterflies are noted for producing a partial extra brood in Cornwall.

CAUSES OF DECLINE OR INCREASE

Nationally, before the last decade, there had been a noticeable reduction in the number of colonies, mainly due to the destruction of habitat, such as scrub encroachment (Asher *et al.* 2001). During that time, though, the butterfly remained reasonably stable in Cornwall. But there was a marked expansion in the early 1990s, as the species adapted to new conditions, although the wet summers of 1997–98 halted and partly reversed this expansion. Now, however, the populations, at least in Cornwall, seem to have recovered.

The larvae are attended by ants (Emmet and Heath 1990), normally *Myrmica sabuleti*, which is common on south-facing, warm coastal slopes, where the grass sward is short, or *Lasius alienus*, the most abundant ant of the sand dunes. Distribution of the ant species probably therefore has a bearing on that of the butterfly.

CONSERVATION

Maintenance of habitats is probably the most important issue, with regular scrub clearance taking place (Spalding with Bourn 2000).

LARVAL FOODPLANTS

On calcareous soils Common Rock Rose (*Helianthemum nummularium*) is normally used, but it is a plant of chalk and limestone regions, and does not occur in Cornwall, where its place as a foodplant is taken by Common Stork's-bill (*Erodium cicutarium*) and Dove's-foot Crane's-bill (*Geranium molle*). The former is especially common on the dunes of Cornwall, while the latter has a more general distribution in the central and western regions of the county; in the east it is mainly confined to coastal areas (French *et al.* 1999). Very occasionally other similar plant species may be used.

ABERRATIONS

Some aberrations are known, mainly involving the colour of the marginal spots on the upper wings, and the arrangement and distinctiveness of those on the undersides. Few have been recorded in Cornwall. Ab. *snelleni*, where the upper black discoidal spots on the forewings are surrounded by white, was recorded at Cremyll in 1862; ab. *pallidior*, with light pink lunules on the upper surfaces, was seen at Penhale in 1993.

Common Blue *Polyommatus icarus*

No. of tetrads (1995–2000): 294
Status in Cornwall: resident
Regional priority: none
Regional rate of change: increasing, +14%

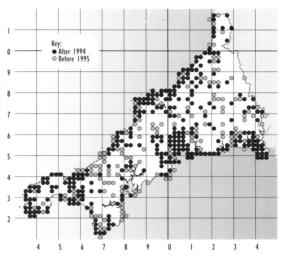

Key:
● After 1994
○ Before 1995

DISTRIBUTION IN CORNWALL

Historically and currently, the Common Blue is one of the most widespread species in the county, although there has been a hint of a decline, albeit in unquantifiable numbers, in areas of development and high-intensity farming. However, the species is known to fluctuate from good to bad years. Fortunately, Cornwall still has large tracts of unimproved, rabbit-grazed grassland where the larval foodplants are abundant. Most of these are now confined to the coastal regions, including St Michael's Mount (Spalding and Tremewan 1998), but even the smallest areas inland often support colonies, although they are nowhere as large as those in the former, where numbers can often be counted in thousands.

HABITAT AND ECOLOGY

The primary habitats of the Common Blue, as indicated above, are in sheltered situations along the coastal grasslands and dunes, on wastelands, heaths and any unimproved grassland with a relatively short sward, which has been grazed by rabbits. But it is seldom found at heights of over 300m. Apart from the huge, coastal populations, most occur in smaller, discrete colonies of a few individuals, or even less.

The butterfly is relatively mobile and can easily form new colonies; it may be met with almost anywhere in Cornwall, including urban gardens, parkland and cemeteries, except on the highest moors.

The larvae in their final stages, as with so many Blues, can be attended by any of three species of ants: *Formica rufa*, *Myrmica sabuleti* and *Lasius alienus* (Emmet and Heath 1990).

The butterfly is normally double-brooded, but in Cornwall a partial third brood usually occurs. The first brood emerges in early May, although specimens have been seen in late April, and continues until the end of June or early July. The second brood emerges in late July and lasts until late September. A partial third brood can be seen flying from mid-September until early to late October, with an overlap

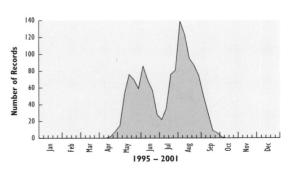

1995 – 2001

between this and the second brood. In many years it is possible to see them on the wing from late April until late October.

CAUSES OF DECLINE OR INCREASE

The main cause for variation in annual numbers is probably the weather in the preceding and current years; generally the warmer and drier the higher the numbers, providing there is no drought, which effects both nectar and foodplants. A more serious decline was brought about in the 1950–1960s when the rabbit population suffered worst from myxomatosis, and grazing to a low sward was reduced. Potential threats are mostly from development and farming.

CONSERVATION

There seems to be little that can be done for such a ubiquitous species, apart from ensuring that its main habitats on dunes and wasteland are correctly managed. Conflicts of interest between one species and another, though, may arise.

LARVAL FOODPLANTS

Most widely used in Cornwall are the Common Bird's-foot Trefoil (*Lotus corniculatus*), which is widespread in the county. Black Medick (*Medicago lupulina*), Lesser Trefoil (*Trifolium dubium*), and White Clover (*Trifolium repens*) can also be used.

ABERRATIONS

Aberrations in this common species are infrequent, especially in Cornwall, although the typical female in many parts of the county has dull blue upper wings in place of the normal brown colouration; in these, the orange lunules on the upper wings are often enhanced (ab. *mariscolore*). These bluish females are said to be more common in chalk and limestone regions, and it is perhaps no coincidence then that the areas where they chiefly occur in Cornwall are on the calcareous dunes. When the female's wings are fully infused with blue, the aberration is called ab. *caerulea*.

A gynandromorph was noted at Boscastle in June 1911 with the left side male and the right side female.

Size variation also occurs in this species: a male 'as large as a Speckled Wood' was seen in July 1991 at St Martin-by-Looe, while a colony of dwarfs was noted at Penlee Point, Rame in the spring of 1990.

Holly Blue *Celestrina argiolus*

No. of tetrads (1995–2000): 246
Status in Cornwall: resident
Regional priority: none
Regional rate of change: fluctuates, but generally increasing, +66%

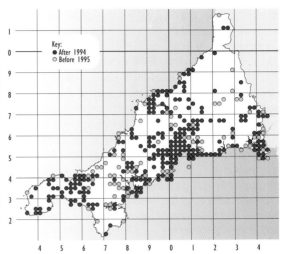

Key:
● After 1994
○ Before 1995

DISTRIBUTION IN CORNWALL

The distribution of this species can vary from widespread to patchy; as explained below, its abundance is cyclical. There is hardly a typical year, but when Holly Blues are plentiful, they can be found almost anywhere in the county, although they tend to favour coastal regions and the valleys leading inland from them. Since it is very mobile and a great wanderer it can also be seen in gardens in urban areas, and in any lanes, tracks and footpaths. The only requirements are ample trees and shrubs containing plenty of the larval foodplants; consequently it is almost entirely absent from treeless and shrubless areas. In intermediate years, which could be said to represent a 'normal' distribution, it may be restricted to certain favoured areas, while in bad years for the species, it seems virtually absent.

The distribution map reflects, not only the Holly Blue, but also the frequency of both observers and foodplants. Inland it is probably spread more widely than is represented on the map.

With the annual fluctuations, the distribution over several years is more difficult to display graphically than perhaps any other British butterfly.

HABITAT AND ECOLOGY

The favourite habitat of the butterfly is anywhere with trees and shrubs containing larval foodplants; here it can be found flying around evergreens in particular and basking, usually fairly high up, on leaves, with its wings half open. It is Britain's only predominately high-flying Blue butterfly, a factor which aids identification. It nectars greedily on holly and ivy blossoms, as well as on the honeydew generated by aphids. The male is sometimes attracted to damp surfaces and animal excreta.

The nominate form does not occur in Britain where its place is taken by subsp. *britanna*; it is also seasonally dimorphic. There are normally two broods, but in Cornwall, in good years, a partial third brood also occurs in some places. The first brood

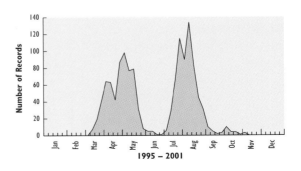

1995 – 2001

emerges in March and April, although specimens have been recorded as early as the beginning of February in the county, and continues until May or early June. In the years of the butterfly's scarcity, specimens of this first brood are rarely seen. The second brood emerges in early July, and there is usually a noticeably short gap between it and the third. The second brood continues until late September. The partial third brood, when it occurs, also begins in late September; specimens of this brood have been seen as late as the end of November, although late October is more normal.

CAUSES OF DECLINE OR INCREASE

As already emphasised the Holly Blue has the most widely fluctuating populations of almost any British species; these fluctuations are cyclical over three to four-year periods, with, most recently, perhaps a longer period of five years when greater numbers were about between 1995–2000. The years with low numbers have been partly blamed on the parasitic ichneumon wasp *Listrodomus nycthemerus*, which is specific to the Holly Blue. It is thought that in years when the butterfly is plentiful, the wasps increase in tandem with it, or at a slightly greater rate, eventually causing a decline in Holly Blues. In turn this also causes a slump in the wasp populations, during which the butterfly recovers, and the cycle is then repeated. But this is not likely to be the only cause especially since the wasp has not apparently been recorded in Cornwall.

Indeed over the past fifteen years or so, the weather may have had an influence, with numbers higher in most hot summers following mild or dry winters, and numbers lower after cold, wet winters. Such winters may also be detrimental to the wasp parasites, which in turn benefits the Holly Blue. Certain geographical areas, which possess micro-climates, may also favour the butterfly; with plentiful larval foodplants, these areas may act as reservoirs for the species in poor years. But the full explanation for the population variations of the Holly Blue has still not been determined.

CONSERVATION

Little can be done to aid the conservation of this species, particularly since the end of the twentieth century not only saw some of the highest numbers for years, but also a considerable expansion of its range. It remains to ensure that there is no shortage of ivy and holly.

LARVAL FOODPLANTS

The Holly Blue is virtually unique among butterflies in requiring totally different larval foodplants for its two main broods. When the first generation, which has reared on ivy, emerges in the spring it searches out Holly (*Ilex aquifolium*), preferably female trees, on which to lay its eggs. The progeny from these, which emerge as the second brood in the summer, return to Ivy (*Hedera helix* ssp. *hibernica* in Cornwall) on which to lay their eggs. The larvae prefer to feed on the buds, flowers or immature berries of these plants. Holly flowers from April to May, although in Cornwall it can be in bloom as early as the preceding November, while ivy flowers from September to November. This difference in flowering time presumably accounts for the Holly Blue's change in taste.

Other species which occasionally have been recorded as larval foodplants include Dogwood (*Cornus sanguinea*), which is rare outside south-east Cornwall; Spindle (*Euonymus europaeus*) which, although commoner that Dogwood, is restricted mainly to the south-east of the county and to areas around the rivers Camel and Fal. European Gorse (*Genista europaeus*) though, may well take the place of Holly on the coast in Cornwall, where the latter seldom occurs, although there is usually plenty of Ivy. The larvae have also been reported on Snowberry (*Symphoricarpos* spp.), although in Cornwall this is a garden escape largely confined to the east of the county.

ABERRATIONS

Aberrations are few in this species, although considerable size variation take place. None have been recorded in Cornwall.

Large Blue *Maculinea arion*

No. of tetrads (1995–2000): 1
Status in Cornwall: re-introduced resident
Regional priority: high
Regional rate of change: increasing

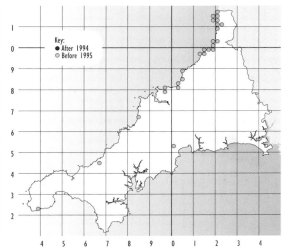

Key:
● After 1994
○ Before 1995

DISTRIBUTION IN CORNWALL

The Large Blue used to be widespread in north Cornwall and probably occupied most of the coastal valleys north-east of Rock; there are also old records from west Penwith. However, Large Blues became extinct in Cornwall in 1973 and nationally in 1979. Despite several claims to the contrary, no secret Large Blue colonies existed after 1973.

Since that time, there has been a national strategy to re-establish the Large Blue in Britain, latterly as part of the Species Recovery Programme funded by English Nature. The national re-establishment programme has been a partnership between the Centre for Ecology and Hydrology, English Nature, the National Trust, Somerset Wildlife Trust, Butterfly Conservation and Gloucestershire Wildlife Trust, co-ordinated by the Joint Committee for the Re-establishment of the Large Blue Butterfly, with scientific advice from Jeremy Thomas. As part of this programme, the Large Blue was introduced using stock from Somerset to a monitored National Trust site on the north Cornwall coast in 2000, when 12 adults (ten females and two males) were put down followed by 300 larvae. Some at least of the adult females laid eggs and several adults were seen in the following summer, the first Cornish Large Blues since 1973.

HABITAT AND ECOLOGY

The Large Blue lays its eggs on the flowers of Wild Thyme (*Thymus polytrichus*), after which the larvae feed inside the flowers. In the fourth instar, the larvae drop to the ground, wait to be collected by red ants and are then taken into nests where larvae feed on ant grubs. The larvae pupate within the nest and the adults emerge the following summer. In Britain, the host ant is *Myrmica sabuleti*, which is widespread in Cornwall on warm south-facing slopes. The habitat therefore has to be suitable for both butterfly and ant. One of the key habitat requirements for *Myrmica sabuleti* is short turf, between 2–4cm high, with abundant bare ground. Other species of red ant such as *Myrmica scabrinodis* will displace *M. sabuleti* on cooler sites. Wild Thyme also does well in these conditions. Optimum habitat conditions are found when each Thyme clump lies within the foraging range of a *M. sabuleti* nest, which is typically 1–2 sq. metres on suitable sites.

CAUSES OF DECLINE OR INCREASE

The Large Blue became extinct in Cornwall due to changing agricultural practices, scrub encroachment and lack of grazing (e.g. by rabbits). Photographs taken in the early 1920s and 1930s of the north coast valleys show short-turf grassland with scattered clumps of gorse; more recent photographs of the same sites show large areas of gorse and blackthorn scrub, with little grassland. Wild Thyme has largely disappeared from these valleys, and generally survives only on the thinner soils at the seaward edges. *Myrmica sabuleti* cannot survive in this dense cool scrub, even on the warm south-facing slopes; as *M. sabuleti* disappeared, so did the Large Blue.

It is too early to say with confidence that the current population in Cornwall is self-maintaining but the outlook is good. It is hoped that more colonies will be established along the north Cornwall coast to ensure that Large Blues will survive here.

Sometime Large Blue habitat at Tidna.

CONSERVATION

The re-establishment of the Large Blue in Cornwall is part of a wider programme of habitat management along the north Atlantic coast. Several valleys are currently under-going targeted management, often as part of Countryside Stewardship schemes, and a number of organisations and private landowners are involved. Management for the Large Blue involves scrub clearance, if possible by burning, followed by grazing by cattle, ponies and/or sheep. Thyme planting is included in the management programme and habitat suitability, which includes sward height, thyme distribution and density of *M. sabuleti*, is monitored regularly as part of the re-introduction programme. The aim is to have three centres with core populations: south of Tintagel, around Morwenstow and near Hartland in Devon. It is hoped that the larger, multi-aspect sites will host large populations from which butterflies may colonise adjacent areas.

Management for Large Blue has been shown to benefit a range of other warmth-loving species, not least the Grayling butterfly (p. 109).

LARVAL FOODPLANTS

In Cornwall only Wild Thyme (*Thymus polytrichus*) is used, although Wild Marjoram (*Origanum vulgare*) may be used in warmer sites in Somerset.

ABERRATIONS

Large Blues are very variable in colour, spotting and size. Russwurm (1978) illustrates seven aberrations from Cornwall, ranging from ab. *artherus* with only the discal spot on each forewing to ab. *insubrica* where the spots are enlarged into streaks. Frohawk (1938) illustrates a specimen of ab. *obsoleta* from Cornwall taken in 1907, without spotting on the underside of the forewings. Large Blues are fully protected by law and therefore aberrations can no longer be collected.

The release of re-introduced Large Blues in 2000; and the Cornish Large Blue, re-introduction.

White Admiral *Limenitis (Ladoga) camilla*

No. of tetrads (1995–2000): 1
Status in Cornwall: doubtful resident; otherwise vagrant
Regional priority: low
Regional rate of change: increasing, +16%

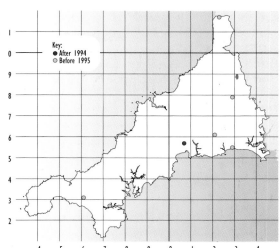

Key:
● After 1994
○ Before 1995

DISTRIBUTION IN CORNWALL

The White Admiral has always been rare in Cornwall, although it had a slightly wider distribution formerly, with appearances near Penzance and at Godolphin. Now its range is much more restricted and the only regular recent sightings in the 1990s were at the Welcombe and Marsland nature reserve. But it was seen near Lewannick in 1969 and at Keveral Wood in 1984, with two more individuals in 1985, one between Luckett and Rame Head and the other at the Deer Park Forest Trail near Herodsfoot. Two other possible sightings were made near Feock in 1998, but the observer also noted that they could have been female Purple Emperors, since he had just witnessed one on the bonnet of his car (p. 122). However another specimen was seen at Pontsmill in 2001 (Lane 2002). It seems possible that in hot years, when backed by easterly winds, individuals move westwards from the Devon valleys into Cornwall.

HABITAT AND ECOLOGY

The butterfly is a woodland species and can be encountered in shady rides and on the edges of sunny glades, especially where bramble blossoms and muddy patches on the ground proliferate, since it seeks nectar from one source and mineral salts from the other. It can tolerate more shade than some other woodland species and consequently can be at home in mature or neglected woods, either deciduous or mixed. It seems to prefer woodlands on damp clay soils, rather than those on chalk or limestone.

The White Admiral is single-brooded, flying from late June until mid-to late August.

CAUSES OF DECLINE OR INCREASE

It is surprising that this butterfly is not commoner in Cornwall, in view of its spread elsewhere (Asher *et al.* 2001). There is no lack of larval foodplant, nor of areas of mature woodland, situated in warm valleys; nor are the woods on calcareous soils.

Perhaps the few specimens seen in the 1980s and 1990s, not far from the south coast, are a welcome portent of things to come. However, high temperatures in June appear to be critical for its survival (Asher *et al.* 2001), and it may be that summer temperatures in Cornwall are generally too low for the butterfly.

CONSERVATION

Much of the conserved woodland in Cornwall is managed in a way to suit various species of fritillary, which usually demand more open habitats. Perhaps it is time to consider leaving some areas moderately neglected to encourage the White Admiral.

LARVAL FOODPLANTS

Apparently the only foodplant known is Honeysuckle (*Lonicera periclymenum*). It prefers to lay its eggs on shady trailing stems, situated 1–2m above the ground.

ABERRATIONS

Aberration in this species is almost always confined to melanism, when the white markings are dusted over, to a greater or lesser extent, by black scalings. None have so far been recorded in Cornwall.

Red Admiral *Vanessa atalanta*

No. of tetrads (1995–2000): 489
Status in Cornwall: migrant and occasional resident
Regional priority: none
Regional rate of change: increasing, +25%

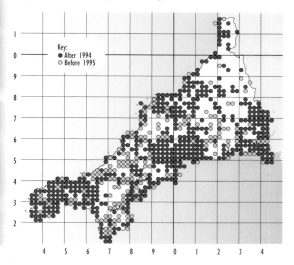

Key:
● After 1994
○ Before 1995

DISTRIBUTION IN CORNWALL

This species is probably the most widely-distributed butterfly in Cornwall, as in much of southern Britain. Although the last decades show records in only about 50% of the tetrads, it must at least have passed through every one, if not pausing within it, because of its migratory habits; even the highest moorland will have been crossed, particularly in good years of immigration. Indeed Cornwall appears to have more than its fair share of the species, since the county seems to be on an immigration route from the Brittany coast to north-east Britain.

In good years waves of immigrants continue into September, many of them producing broods in Britain. Thousands of these home-bred specimens then join other emigrants moving south from August onwards; perhaps meeting unfavourable winds, they tend to veer to the west on reaching the coast, when hundreds can be seen westering along it in the autumn. Many of these fail to make the journey across the Channel, and attempt to over-winter, but few probably survive; there is, though, ample evidence in recent years that some do (Tucker 1991).

Because of its habits, the butterfly's distribution has a strong coastal bias, especially in the autumn. Both immigrants and emigrants usually pause to 'refuel' on nectar sources when they reach the coast, either following a cross-Channel journey, or in anticipation of a return.

HABITAT AND ECOLOGY

Despite many coastal sightings, the species is a woodland, orchard, hedgerow and garden butterfly. Here, newly-arrived males and British-bred individuals take up territories looking for mates. Surprisingly for such a common species, there are only two occasions in Britain, both of which were in Cornwall, when the butterfly has been seen mating. The first recorded instance was in a stableyard in north Cornwall in early December 1984; the temperature was 12°C (54°F) and the time between noon and 13.15 hours. Four Red Admirals were seen basking or flying round the yard; after half an hour of this activity, a male

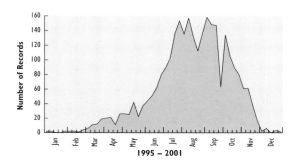

and female began a courtship chase, the latter leading the male high around trees and low over the yard. Eventually they settled on a shaded tree branch some 6m above the ground where the male was successful in mating; they were still in coition at 15.15 hours (Archer-Lock 1989). Apart from being a first record in Britain of mating Red Admirals, it is also the sole instance of winter-mating in this country.

More recently in April 2001, another pair were witnessed in Camborne just completing their courtship chase, and then settling, again in the shade, to mate, where they remained for up to an hour (Harris 2003).

The overall ecology is complex. Egg-laying has been seen as late as mid-November in the south-east of Britain, and is suspected in December in Cornwall. Larvae in all stages of development can be seen here in late autumn, so it would appear that the Red Admiral can over-winter at any of its stages – egg, larva, pupa or adult.

The flight period is consequently a little confused. Over-wintered adults may survive into March, or more rarely April, so that a slight overlap occurs between them and the first immigrants; but only about 5% of the annual migrant total arrive between March and May. From June to September successive waves of immigrants in their hundreds or even thousands fly in, often continuing into November. Meanwhile British broods are being produced, which tend to fly south in the opposite direction so as to become emigrants. Thus the butterflies become intermixed, although they can usually be told apart by the direction of flight: immigrants fly north-east and emigrants south.

In sum, therefore, there is no mild, sunny and calm day in the year when a Red Admiral could not be seen in Cornwall.

CAUSES OF DECLINE OR INCREASE

The species would appear to be on the increase. The annual British populations of this migrating butterfly are controlled by the varying weather on the continent and in the Mediterranean basin; cold or wet weather there may mean delayed flight or low numbers arriving in Britain. Nevertheless, Cornwall usually receives sufficient butterflies from which sizeable populations can breed; but even here a cold, wet summer may prevent such a recovery. As with most butterflies long, warm summers favour high populations.

CONSERVATION

No specific methods of conservation are needed for this species, although it would be aided if gardeners left a patch of nettles uncut in a corner of their plots. Since the butterfly prefers fresh, young leaves, cutting the nettles to the ground once in midsummer will ensure a good supply.

LARVAL FOODPLANTS

The Common Nettle (*Urtica dioica*) is most frequently used, but Small Nettle (*Urtica urens*) will suffice, although it is infrequent in Cornwall and largely restricted to the west of the county. Pellitory-of-the-wall (*Parietaria judaica*) and Hop (*Humulus lupulus*) have also been recorded; the former is mainly confined to coastal regions in the county, while the latter is scarce.

ABERRATIONS

Aberrations are rare and only a few have been recorded in Cornwall. A specimen of ab. *klemensiewiczi* was captured at Gwithian in August 1983; in this the black spots on the red bands of the hindwings are missing (Tucker 1991). An aberration ab. *millierei*, where the red bands are replaced by white was photographed at Mylor in May 1990, while a specimen where only the band on the right hindwing was affected (ab. *semi-millierei*?) was seen near Hayle at the end of July 2000.

Painted Lady *Vanessa (Cynthia) cardui*

No. of tetrads (1995–2000): 352
Status in Cornwall: immigrant and rarely a resident
Regional priority: none
Regional rate of change: not assessed

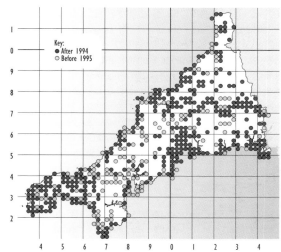

Key:
● After 1994
○ Before 1995

DISTRIBUTION IN CORNWALL

Although a considerably less-frequent immigrant than the Red Admiral, with much more variable numbers, in most years the Painted Lady is not uncommon in the county. It is continuously brooded in its nearest homelands of north Africa, whence it has become an inveterate traveller. Consequently, it is widely distributed in the county. In any one year, it may be recorded in only a quarter of the county's tetrads (due to a lack of recorders), or, as in 1999, even less. But in the invasion years, such as 1996 when millions entered Britain on a broad front, some must have flown over every coastal and inland tetrad in Cornwall. In that year the main influx occurred in only a few weeks during the first part of June; over 1,000 were counted coming in from the sea at Rinsey within an hour, on a front only 10m wide. But the vast numbers then seen appeared reluctant to go to sea again, for, although very many quickly reached the north coast of Cornwall, only one was seen on a visit to south Wales in mid-June.

Another reasonably good period was 2000–01 when a number were sighted during the winter, with indications of immigration in December (Lane 2001). In sum though, over a ten-year period, every area of Cornwall is likely to be visited.

Even in normal years, with far fewer numbers, most tetrads should be frequented at some time, since, as with the Red Admiral, the western part of the county seems to be on a migration route from the coast of Brittany to north-eastern Britain. But in sparse years, as in 1999 when only a few hundred were recorded nationally, very few tetrads in Cornwall were visited.

The butterfly tends to follow coastlines on migration, so that their frequency on the coast can be somewhat higher than inland. Mainly southerly winds from north Africa are responsible for the major proportion of Cornish specimens, but it has been known to invade from the east, as in 1980, when only a few adults reached the county.

As with the Red Admiral, Cornish broods of this butterfly tend to join the flights of emigrants in the autumn, when they can intermix with late immigrants. In 1996, hundreds were seen flying south and gathering on coastal sites before setting off on their journey across the Channel (*contra* Asher *et al.* 2001).

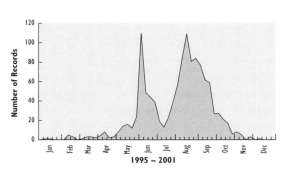

1995 – 2001

HABITAT AND ECOLOGY

The Painted Lady can be found almost anywhere in its relentless search for nectar, larval foodplants and mates; any warm, flower-rich area, be it cliff-top or urban garden will provide its quota in years of abundance, especially after the first British brood has emerged.

After mating, females frequent thistle patches which provide larval foodplants and, later in the season, nectar. It is surprisingly tolerant of windy places and can be drawn to thistles on exposed hillsides. Other attractive nectar sources for both sexes are Privet (*Ligustrum vulgare*), Buddleja (*Buddleja davidii*) and Ivy (*Hedara helix* ssp. *hibernica*) blossoms.

The flight pattern of the butterfly, as with the Red Admiral, is complicated owing to its continuous breeding habit; the whole life cycle can be completed in as little as a month (Asher *et al*. 2001) with no hibernating period recognised, and it has been recorded in every month of the year in Cornwall. Normally though, the earliest migrants arrive in May or June and produce a British brood, which emerges in July and August, when the butterfly is most abundant. In very favourable summers, a second and even possibly a third brood also reaches maturity; the progeny mostly must join any survivors of the first brood who attempt to emigrate. But what of the earlier stages of the butterfly's development any or all of which could be present and which have not reached maturity? Received opinion says that they cannot survive the British winter, and certainly there is no evidence for a subsequent 'spring brood'. Yet in late October 1997 a freshly-emerged specimen was captured near Hayle, marked and released. This re-emerged in early April of the following year, and was then seen intermittently until the middle of May (Wacher 1998c). So at least the adult butterfly is capable of surviving the Cornish winter although the occasions when it happens are probably few; evidence is still lacking for the over-wintering of eggs, larvae or pupae.

CAUSES OF DECLINE OR INCREASE

The variation in numbers from year to year is related to climatic conditions in north Africa and the Mediterranean region, and also to the breeding success on the desert fringes of the former; abnormal rainfall there provides lush and ample larval foodplant which promotes populations. But events such as unseasonable thunderstorms in the middle of a migration can kill many thousands of adults in flight.

CONSERVATION

Apart from leaving an uncut growth of thistles in field corners, on headlands and in gardens, little can be done to aid the conservation of this species.

LARVAL FOODPLANTS

Various species of thistle, including Spear Thistle (*Cirsium vulgare*), Creeping Thistle (*Cirsium arvense*) and Marsh Thistle (*Cirsium palustre*) are most used, all of which are common on Cornwall, but almost any species of the *Cirsium* or *Carduus* families will suffice. It is also known to lay eggs on Viper's-bugloss (*Echium vulgare*) which is restricted to the dunes of north Cornwall, Mallow species (*Malva* spp.) and even Nettles (*Urtica* spp.). In 1996 a nearly fully-grown caterpillar was found on a Globe Artichoke (*Cynara scolymus*) in a garden near Hayle.

ABERRATIONS

Aberrations are rare in the Painted Lady and they have seldom been recorded in Cornwall. A specimen of ab. *varini* was captured at Carharrack in 1947; in this the submarginal spots on the hindwings are elongated. More common is ab. *pallida*, where the ground colour is a paler pink on smaller specimens; one was seen at Portholland in January 1988, another at the Lizard in November 1994, and most recently a third at Portmellon, Mevagissey in March 2000.

Painted Lady ab. *pallida*.

Small Tortoiseshell *Aglais urticae*

No. of tetrads (1995–2000): 366
Status in Cornwall: resident and migrant
Regional priority: none
Regional rate of change: increasing, +51%

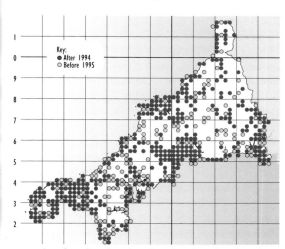

Key:
● After 1994
○ Before 1995

DISTRIBUTION IN CORNWALL

The Small Tortoiseshell is widespread and common throughout most of Cornwall, although given to periodic fluctuations in populations. As with other closely-related species, the home-bred butterflies are reinforced by migrants; it is a great traveller and specimens have been recorded up to 150km from the point of release (Roer 1968).

In the west of the county, numbers were much reduced in the late 1990s, and the butterfly became almost scarce. Numbers recovered, however, in 2000–2002; they were obviously more resistant than other species to the cold, wet May and June of the former year. This fact has been confirmed by laboratory research (Asher *et al*. 2001); the butterfly is once again a common sight.

HABITAT AND ECOLOGY

The adult butterfly can be met with almost anywhere in urban gardens, lanes, fields, waste land and dunes, wherever there are larval foodplants and an abundance of nectar sources. However its wandering habits can take it into city centres and to the tops of the highest moors in Cornwall

The Small Tortoiseshell's flight periods are complicated and affected by both climatic conditions and geographical situation. It over-winters as the adult and it can often be found sheltering in houses and sheds during the winter months. But a sudden warm day or too much central-heating can reactivate them, when they again take to the wing. It is doubtful if these specimens, so awakened and released into the open air, manage to survive for any length of time. More normally, hibernating adults emerge in Cornwall from March onwards, depending on the weather; they then mate and lay eggs, which produce the first brood in late June and July. What happens subsequently depends on the weather and on the length of the days. The latter will determine whether the adults so produced will breed again immediately, or will enter hibernation straight away and reproduce the following year; if they breed, a second generation is in flight from late August onwards (Asher *et al*. 2001). In very favourable

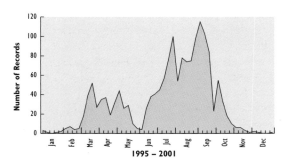

1995 – 2001

years, and in particular in Cornwall, it is possible that a third brood can occur, otherwise the progeny from the second generation enter hibernation.

This flight pattern is further complicated by incoming migrants in early spring and summer, which presumably set up their own breeding sequence on arrival, which may or may not synchronise with the home-bred adults. While there is evidence that autumn shows a southward drift of the species, there is apparently none to show whether immigrants can successfully over-winter in Britain, or even whether they achieve a return to the continent.

CAUSES OF DECLINE OR INCREASE

Figures show a very considerable recent increase, perhaps marred somewhat by those for the late 1990s, although that has now been shown to be one of the periodic fluctuations to which the butterfly is subject. Overall its populations are probably stable nationally, but seem to be increasing in Cornwall.

The larvae in their final stages of development can be attacked by the Tachinid Fly (*Phryxe vulgaris*). Fortunately for the Small Tortoiseshell this insect is restricted mainly to the coastal regions in Cornwall.

CONSERVATION

As with other closely-related species, the maintenance of good patches of larval foodplant is a necessary aid to conservation.

LARVAL FOODPLANTS

Common Nettle (*Urtica dioica*) and Small Nettle (*Urtica urens*) seem to be the only plants used; small plants on the sunniest and warmest side of large clumps are most favoured. As previously mentioned Small Nettle is mainly restricted to west Cornwall, where it is infrequent.

It would seem that the increased use of nitrogenous fertilisers has promoted the growth of lusher clumps of nettles, which in turn probably benefit the butterfly, so that it can easily proliferate in areas of intensive agriculture.

ABERRATIONS

There is a great deal of variation in this species, and extreme forms are less rare than in most (Russworm 1978); several have been seen in Cornwall. A very pale form with a pinkish ground colour, ab. *lutea*, was captured at Boscastle in June 1955, and an albino, ab. *pallida*, was seen at Perranporth in July 1958. Ab. *ichnusoides*, where the two black spots on the forewings are greatly reduced in size, was observed at Wheal Rose, Scorrier in July 1945 and again in August 1956. An example with no spots was seen in the locality in 1969.

Large Tortoiseshell *Nymphalis polychloros*

No. of tetrads (1995–2000): 3
Status in Cornwall: extinct, possibly rare migrant
Regional priority: none
Regional rate of change: not assessed

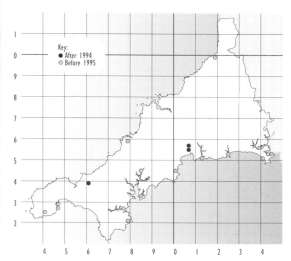

Key:
● After 1994
◎ Before 1995

DISTRIBUTION IN CORNWALL

This butterfly is probably no longer resident in Britain, and probably never has been in Cornwall, owing to the scarcity of its larval foodplant. Indeed it may never have been more than a temporary resident in this country, being dependant on fresh immigrations to maintain its populations (Chalmers-Hunt and Owen 1953), which have always been subject to considerable fluctuations. It occurs more frequently in the south-east and its appearances in Cornwall have always been fitful, the first record being at Falmouth in 1849. Since then there have been spasmodic sightings in the following years (numbers in brackets), mostly near the south coast but stretching the full length of the county: 1893 (1), 1902 (?), 1903 (?), 1918 (1), 1935 (2), 1936 (1), 1943 (1), 1945 (2), 1946 (1), 1948 (1), ? 1955 (1), 1980 (2), ?1981 (1), 1984 (1). Since then there has been an unconfirmed but probable sighting near Hayle in August 1999, and a confirmed appearance of an over-wintered specimen at Pontsmill, near St Austell in March 2000 (Lane 2000a).

HABITAT AND ECOLOGY

The Large Tortoiseshell is capable of surviving the British winter and hibernates as the adult. It is essentially a woodland butterfly, although it ranges widely with only one or two seen at the same time; consequently it can be found in hedgerows and gardens. Two out of the three specimens seen in Kent in 1942, were nectaring on garden buddleja, and it has been recorded on other garden flowers.

Normally there is only one brood, commonly in July and August, and the butterflies enter hibernation early; one was recorded doing so as early as the first week in July. It is probable that the adults do not mate until the following spring.

CAUSES OF DECLINE OR INCREASE

The butterfly has always been subject to periodic decline and recovery, and the last significant recovery was in the 1940s, followed by a decline. It cannot then be related to the advent of Dutch Elm Disease, which did not occur until the 1970s, although the subsequent death of so many trees cannot have aided its recovery in Britain. But in Cornwall its main larval foodplant has always been scarce. One reason for its decline may be a higher incidence of a parasitic wasp (*Psychophagus omnivorus*) although there are no records of this species in Cornwall.

CONSERVATION

There is little that can be done to aid this species.

LARVAL FOODPLANTS

Common English Elm (*Ulmus procera*) and Wych Elm (*Ulmus glabra*) were the most favoured, which are respectively rare and scarce in Cornwall. It is not known if the Cornish Elm (*Ulmus minor* ssp. *angustifolia*) is a suitable substitute.

ABERRATIONS

Aberrations are rare in this species and none have been recorded in Cornwall.

Camberwell Beauty *Nymphalis antiopa*

No. of tetrads (1995–2000): 3
Status in Cornwall: rare immigrant
Regional priority: none
Regional rate of change: not assessed

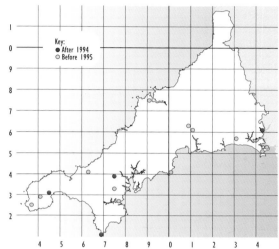

Key:
● After 1994
○ Before 1995

DISTRIBUTION IN CORNWALL

The Camberwell Beauty is not known to breed in Britain and mainly reaches this country as a migrant from Scandinavia; consequently it is most commonly seen in eastern counties. But every now and again, specimens, possibly aided by a fair wind, overshoot and end up in Cornwall. About 16 have been recorded from different parts of the county in the last century up to 1990 (numbers in brackets); 1901 (1); 1927 (6); 1947 (3); 1949 (1); 1973 (1); 1976 (1); 1979 (1); 1983 (1); 1989 (1). In the last decade or so, one was seen in 1990 east of Penryn, with an unconfirmed sighting of another in 1994 just north-east of Stithians; whether this is the same one that was seen not far away, near Burncoose Nurseries, either in 1994 or 1995 cannot now be ascertained. In 1995 two were observed, one near Lizard Point and the other at Landulph Marsh, north of Saltash. Finally one was reported at Madron, near Penzance in 2000. None have been seen since then, and there must always be a suspicion that the specimens have been captive-bred and released.

HABITAT AND ECOLOGY

In Europe and Scandinavia the butterfly is normally a woodland species, but on its migratory flights, when it is usually seen in Cornwall, it can be found almost anywhere, but especially on garden or wayside flowers and on rotten fruit.

In Europe there is a single brood, which emerges later in Scandinavia than in southern countries, and is normally on the wing through August and September, when most British examples are reported; however there is not a month of the year when it has not been seen.

The butterfly hibernates as the adult and some individuals have been recorded in the spring suggesting that the occasional specimen survives the British winter successfully. The six which were supposedly found in a hole in a stone wall in north Cornwall in August 1927 may have been an early attempt to hibernate.

CAUSES OF DECLINE OR INCREASE

The Camberwell Beauty seems unable to establish itself as a British breeding species, probably because the winters are too mild and damp for the adults to survive them successfully.

Years with enhanced migrations are usually due to stable high pressure systems in August over the North Sea, producing north-easterly or easterly winds from Scandinavia flowing to south-east Britain.

CONSERVATION

No specific conservation methods are needed of this species.

LARVAL FOODPLANTS

Various trees and bushes are used as larval foodplants on the continent, among which are Willows (*Salix* spp.), Poplars (*Populus* spp.), Elms (*Ulmus* spp.) and Birch (*Betula* spp.); poplars are scarce in Cornwall.

ABERRATIONS

None have been recorded in Cornwall.

Peacock *Inarchis io*

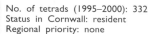

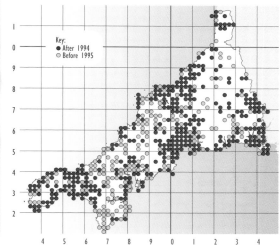

No. of tetrads (1995–2000): 332
Status in Cornwall: resident
Regional priority: none
Regional rate of change: increasing, +14%

Key:
● After 1994
○ Before 1995

DISTRIBUTION IN CORNWALL

The Peacock is widespread over the whole county, although, like most butterflies, it avoids the higher ground. The distribution map, as with so many common species, shows more where there are recorders than butterflies; nevertheless the species is subject to fluctuations and from a decline in the mid-1990s has become increasingly common in the last two years.

HABITAT AND ECOLOGY

The butterfly can be observed in woodland glades and rides, on scrubland, waste ground, hedgerows and in gardens, wherever there are nectar sources and larval foodplants; brambles, thistles and several cultivated flower species are attractive, including Sedum (*Sedum* spp.), Buddleja (*Buddleja* spp.) and Michaelmas Daisies (*Aster* spp.). But above all, it is drawn to Hemp Agrimony (*Eupatorium cannabinum*) and a single clump can often be host to a dozen or more butterflies.

The Peacock is normally single-brooded, although in very hot summers, a partial second brood occurs. It over-winters as the adult, which tends to enter hibernation as early as August, and spends the winter in any dark place, such as holes in trees, but is less commonly seen in houses than the Small Tortoiseshell. Any warm, sunny winter's day in December, January or February can reactivate the butterflies, especially in Cornwall where such days are not infrequent, but the main peak of emergences occurs in late March and April, when mating and egg-laying take place. In very hot years there can then be accelerated development which is promoted by the long daylight hours of midsummer (Asher *et al.* 2001), so that adults emerge in early June and then go on to produce a partial second brood in the late autumn. Under normal conditions, though, the progeny of the hibernators appear in late July and eventually seek their own winter quarters. Thus, but for a very short time in June, it is possible to see a Peacock during any month of the year. Since it is a mobile species and can fly considerable distances, it is possible that some migration occurs.

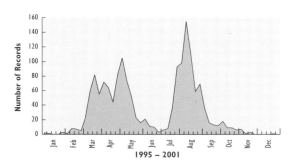

1995 – 2001

CAUSES OF DECLINE OR INCREASE

A wet summer will cause a slump in populations, but recovery usually seems to be fairly rapid in following seasons. Over the years there has probably been an increase in abundance. Intensive agriculture is a potential threat, particularly where sprays are used to eliminate the foodplant.

CONSERVATION

So long as the extensive network of footpaths and bridleways with their Cornish hedges and ample foodplants exist, the Peacock will probably continue to flourish in the county.

LARVAL FOODPLANTS

The Common Nettle (*Urtica dioica*) seems to be the principal foodplant. Occasional use of Small Nettle (*Urtica urens*) and Hop (*Humulus lupulus*) have been recorded, but both are uncommon in Cornwall.

Large nettle clumps are chosen, in sheltered positions in full sun, and situated on woodland edges or south-facing hedgerows.

ABERRATIONS

Aberrations are rare, and very few have been recorded in Cornwall. A specimen taken in Sheviock Wood near St Germans in August 1962 had the red colouration replaced by a dull straw, perhaps ab. *fulva*, while one from Godolphin had only the right forewing so coloured. Dwarf specimens have been reported in the Liskeard area.

Comma *Polygonia c-album*

No. of tetrads (1995–2000): 94
Status in Cornwall: resident
Regional priority: none
Regional rate of change: increasing, +39%

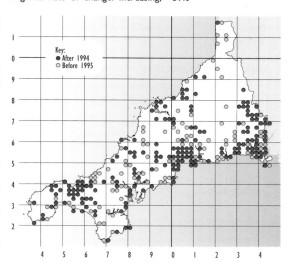

Key:
● After 1994
○ Before 1995

DISTRIBUTION IN CORNWALL

During the late nineteenth and early twentieth centuries the Comma suffered a serious decline being, in the end, restricted to a few counties along the southern Welsh Marches. During this period, the butterfly was unknown in Cornwall, although there are two records from Devon. But a recovery began about 1914 and the Comma gradually spread over the whole of southern England. The writer well remembers the excitement caused by its appearance near Broadstairs, Kent in 1939, almost as far east as it could go, although it had appeared in east Cornwall slightly earlier at Polyphant in 1933, after a prolonged march through Devon in the late 1920s (Bracken 1936). By 1935 it had travelled further west and reached Redruth, with Hayle and Marazion in the following year. Since then it has gradually become widespread throughout Cornwall, although remaining scarce in the far west of the county; nevertheless it seems generally to have avoided the higher ground of Bodmin Moor, Carnmenellis and the moors of west Penwith. In the last decade or so numbers recorded in the west have increased and it appeared at St Just-in-Penwith in 1994. The Comma's relative progress can be measured by comparing distribution maps for each decade since 1969. Certainly it is more frequently seen just east of Hayle, where none appeared in 1994–96, but the ensuing years saw permanent populations well established.

Finally it is worth mentioning that the Comma must be almost the only butterfly in Cornwall to have an official maritime recording. In the 1970s a specimen was sighted from a boat 3.5km off Botallack Head. This would explain the handful of records from the Isles of Scilly, where, as yet, it is not thought to breed. It is also one of the few butterflies to show nocturnal activity and one was seen at a mercury vapour lamp in September 1984 at Downderry, although migrating Red Admirals can also be attracted, as at Loe Bar in 1987.

HABITAT AND ECOLOGY

The butterfly is essentially a woodland species, but its strong flight and wandering habits mean that it can also be seen in tree-lined lanes, trackways, scrubland and gardens, where it is attracted by Buddleja (*Buddleja* spp.), Michaelmas Daisies

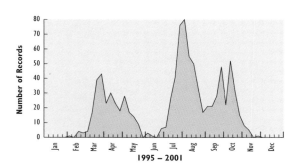

1995 – 2001

(*Aster* spp.) and even rotting fruit. The pre-hibernation specimens also enjoy brambles (*Rubus* spp.), Ivy (*Hedera* spp.) and Hemp Agrimony (*Eupatorium cannabinum*).

The flight pattern is complicated, with a main brood in late June to early August and a partial second brood from late August to early October, but within these two broods there are variations in the life history of the butterfly. It over-winters as the adult and has reappeared as early as February in Cornwall, but mainly in late March and April, when mating occurs. The first generation so produced in late June exhibit two types of lifestyle. Some mate quickly and are the source of the second generation in late summer. Those that show no signs of mating behaviour probably take longer to mature and, when adult, concentrate on nectaring in a more leisurely way, and ultimately hibernate. It has been claimed (Harper and Waller 1950) that succulence of the foodplants controls the rate of larval development, although temperature and day length are also apparently governing factors (Asher *et al*. 2001); but it must be admitted that full understanding of the Comma's development has not yet been achieved. Those that develop rapidly are different in appearance from the others of the midsummer brood. Their upper wings are paler in colour and the wing margins less scalloped; it is recognised as form *hutchinsoni*. Thus the butterflies that reappear in the following spring are a mixture of the unmated first brood with those of the second generation.

CAUSES OF DECLINE OR INCREASE

Cornwall has seen a very definite increase both in numbers and geographical distribution in the last decades, but even then climatic conditions can cause a temporary decline. A cold, wet winter such as 2000–01 saw a marked decline of hibernators reappearing in the spring.

CONSERVATION

No specific methods of conservation are considered necessary for this species.

LARVAL FOODPLANTS

During the nineteenth century, the principal foodplant seems to have been Hop (*Humulus lupulus*). But with the decline of hop-growing in England, it has changed to Common Nettle (*Urtica dioica*), although Elms (*Ulmus* spp.) and Currants (*Ribes* spp.) have been recorded. Prominent clumps or shrubs in the shelter of woodland edges and hedgerows are most favoured.

ABERRATIONS

F. *hutchinsoni*, which is the best known, is restricted to the midsummer generation; their offspring are normal. Several other aberrations are known, but none have yet been recorded in Cornwall.

Small Pearl-bordered Fritillary *Boloria selene*

No. of tetrads (1995–2000): 65
Status in Cornwall: resident
Regional priority: medium
Regional rate of change: increasing, +23%

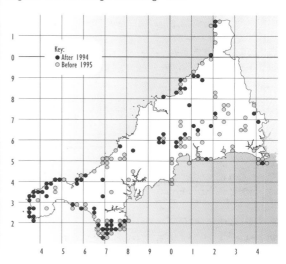

Key:
● After 1994
◉ Before 1995

DISTRIBUTION IN CORNWALL

The Small Pearl-bordered Fritillary is still locally common and widespread in parts of Cornwall, notably the Lizard peninsula and the far west, where it is mostly restricted to the coastal regions and exists in small colonies. There is a scattering of colonies along the north coast on the dunes and in the valleys between Hayle and Bude, and a couple of isolated ones on the south coast between Fowey and Rame Head. Inland, the sites are more scattered, with the principal concentration stretching eastward from Goss Moor by way of Breney Common nature reserve to beyond Bodmin. The Goss Moor national nature reserve has the largest populations in Cornwall. Additionally they are also found at the Marsland and Luckett nature reserves.

HABITAT AND ECOLOGY

The butterfly is said to populate four main types of habitat (Asher *et al.* 2001). In Cornwall these are now largely reduced to two with one other addition, since the woodland colonies have mostly died out. On the coast in west Cornwall and the Lizard, it inhabits damp grassland, open bracken scrub which replicates woodland and heathland, but is also found on the dunes between Hayle and Gwithian, and at Gear Sands. Inland, grassland especially damp grassy heath with bracken and scrub is favoured; but a certain amount of grazing to check the uncontrolled growth of this bracken and scrub is considered essential. Perhaps the Small Pearl-bordered Fritillary's ability to adapt to a variety of non-woodland habitats in Cornwall will enable it to survive, and prevent any further decline in the species.

The nominate subspecies *Boloria selene selene* is found in most of Britain, although it is replaced by subsp. *insularum* in Scotland and the inner western isles. It is sometimes found flying in company with the Pearl-bordered Fritillary (p. 89), although the latter emerges slightly earlier; when this happens, problems of identification can arise.

The butterfly is normally single brooded and is on the wing from early May (occasionally late April) until June in the county. A partial second brood is said to occur sometimes in parts of

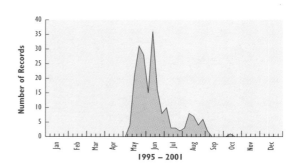

1995 – 2001

southern England and south Wales, but in Cornwall this happens almost every year, especially on the dunes and in the north coast valleys, with a flight period from early August until early September; this brood often outnumbers the first on the Towans east of Hayle, and certainly greater numbers were seen flying in August than in May in the two years 2000–01.

CAUSES OF DECLINE OR INCREASE
Destruction of habitat is the prime cause of the extinction of colonies, whether by agricultural improvement, overgrazing, growth of scrub or changes to woodland management.

CONSERVATION
Fortunately for this butterfly, most of the areas which it now inhabits are owned or leased by conservation bodies, such as the Cornwall Wildlife Trust and the National Trust; the latter owns many of the coastal sites on which it is found. But even then, care must be exercised to prevent the over-enthusiastic tidying-up of old industrial wastelands.

LARVAL FOODPLANTS
The commonest foodplant is Common Dog-violet (*Viola riviniana*), which occurs widely in Cornwall. Marsh Violet (*Viola palustris* ssp. *juressi*) is also used, and is the favoured foodplant in the mid-Cornwall moors and Bodmin Moor. Other violets may sometimes be considered, but they are usually rejected by the egg-laying female. Medium-sized plants growing in damp, open, sunny situations are usually chosen, in contrast to the Pearl-bordered Fritillary which prefers drier conditions.

ABERRATIONS
Russwurm (1978) claims that aberration is more frequent in this than in other British fritillaries, whereas Emmet and Heath (1990) state that it is rare. In extreme forms, confusion with those of the Pearl-bordered Fritillary creates identification problems. Some aberrations, but not many, have been recorded in Cornwall. Frohawk (1938) illustrates ab. *margostriata*, in which the sub-marginal spots are replaced by bars, and which was taken in 'north Cornwall' in 1937. Another specimen of this aberration was recorded near Perranporth in June 1964. It has been claimed that second-brood specimens are much smaller than those of the first brood (Tremewan 1956) and certainly a diminutive example was seen at Upton Towans in late August 2000; it was scarcely larger than a Duke of Burgundy. But in general the distinction does not seem to apply.

Small Pearl-bordered Fritillary, underside.

Pearl-bordered Fritillary, underside.

Pearl-bordered Fritillary *Boloria euphrosyne*

No. of tetrads (1995–2000): 21
Status in Cornwall: resident
Regional priority: high
Regional rate of change: decreasing, -2%

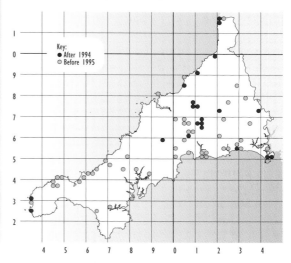

Key:
● After 1994
○ Before 1995

DISTRIBUTION IN CORNWALL

This butterfly is now comparatively rare in Cornwall, although once it was widespread; the decline is not only in the county, but also has been recorded nationally, and it is one of the most rapidly diminishing species in Britain. The remaining sites in the county where it is found are in central and northern parts, with the western edge of Bodmin Moor supporting good populations; there are also isolated colonies in south-eastern Cornwall, according to recent fieldwork, and one exists at Millendreath, near Looe. Unless any new evidence comes to light, this delightful species must now be considered extinct in western Cornwall, despite some records in the Land's End and St Just areas. Some doubt has been expressed about the authenticity of these records (Penhallurick 1996) and, although a number of people have searched likely areas in the last few years no confirmation can be provided, but small colonies may still survive in out-of-the-way places. The largest known colony in the county is in the north at the Marsland nature reserve near the Devon border.

It is now represented in few tetrads, with seldom more than one or two colonies in any; in sum the county can only account for at the most ten colonies, so there is no room for complacency.

HABITAT AND ECOLOGY

The primary habitat of the Pearl-bordered Fritillary in Cornwall is now bracken-covered, south-facing hillsides, which are lightly grazed and adjoin old remnant woodland. A few small populations occur on the south coast near Looe, where the habitat is open steep slopes with abundant litter of shale; shelter from the strong sea breezes is provided by sycamore scrub.

It is a relatively weak-flying, but sun-loving, butterfly, and prefers the shelter of dells, glades and combes with low ground cover and an abundance of its larval foodplant; more exposed sites are seldom chosen, unless they are facing south or south-west.

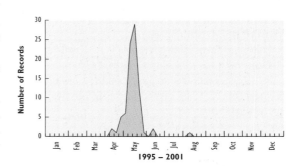

1995 – 2001

It sometimes shares similar habitats with the more common Small Pearl-bordered Fritillary (p. 87), which flies faster and is more wide-ranging; the latter butterfly also appears a little later in the season, when most Pearl-bordered Fritillaries are past their best. The presence of early Small Pearl-bordered Fritillaries, especially in west Cornwall may cause confusion between the two species and may have led to false claims of sightings of this species. Unlike its near relative, it does not seem able to adapt to new or changing habitats.

The adult butterfly normally emerges in the first week of May, but specimens can be about in April, and there is even one recorded in March; it is the earliest of the fritillaries to emerge and its flight period lasts until June. There is in Cornwall an occasional, partial second brood in August and early September, and an example was seen in late August 1948 at Porthtowan, with another at Marsland in September 1988 and, most recently in September 1991, at Hawks Tor, North Hill.

CAUSES OF DECLINE OR INCREASE
The causes for its decline can be either gradual or rapid, and are linked to the weather. Gradual destruction of habitat is caused by the cessation of grazing, leading to the uncontrolled encroachment of scrub; equally, overgrazing and 'poaching' on grassland can destroy the larval foodplants; decline in coppicing can lead to their shading-out. Rapid destruction of habitat can be caused by large-scale and repeated burning, or by bracken eradication measures. Since the species prefers well-drained drier terrain, a succession of wet springs and summers can be detrimental, whereas a hot spring, as in 1997, promotes a temporary expansion in numbers of adults.

CONSERVATION
Conservation for this species in the present agricultural climate now depends on management, which should be finely balanced between extremes, and varies according to the habitat type. In woodland, periodic coppicing is necessary, coupled perhaps with the control of any resulting bracken and excess herbage. Felling of trees in adjacent areas, with the consequent growth of a ground flora, allows this not very mobile butterfly to move from one which is being shaded out by tree growth, to another where the ground flora has just been renewed.

In a bracken habitat, where scrub, especially gorse, also occurs, control is needed to provide the sheltered glades and rides, where the larval foodplant can grow in abundance, in conjunction with sufficient dead bracken and leaf litter, on which most of the eggs are laid. Control can be exercised by light grazing by ponies or stock, or by periodic manual clearance (Spalding with Bourn 2000).

A new initiative has now been set up (2002) in the county by the Cornwall Fritillary Group, with funding from English Nature, to monitor and assess the Pearl-bordered Fritillary's status in Cornwall; if potential sites can be identified, re-introduction might be considered at one of them (Spalding with Bourn 2000). The survey should provide information on habitat management, especially in connection with scrub-clearance at the colony near Looe.

English Nature has extended the boundary of the Camel Special Area of Conservation (SAC) to include a good example of a colony near St Breward.

LARVAL FOODPLANTS
The commonest foodplant is the Common Dog-violet (*Viola riviniana*), although it is possible that other violets may be used from time-to-time, including the Marsh Violet (*Viola palustris*), which tends to coincide in Cornwall with the butterfly's colonies.

ABERRATIONS
Aberrations are rather less frequent than in the Small Pearl-bordered Fritillary. A variation of ab. *stramineus*, when the pale colour of the aberration was reduced to a pale cream blotch on the upperside of each hindwing, was recorded at Park Shady, Porthtowan in May 1955; another was seen at Newmills as recently as May 2000. A male ab. *pittionii*, a partly melanic form, was seen at Tuckingmill in May 1994, and another male with hindwings approaching ab. *vanescens* was noted in the now-extinct colony at Keveral Wood in May 1991.

Queen of Spain Fritillary *Issoria (Argynnis) lathonia*

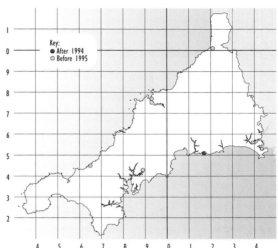

No. of tetrads (1995–2000): 1
Status in Cornwall: very rare migrant
Regional priority: none
Regional rate of change: not assessed

Key:
● After 1994
○ Before 1995

DISTRIBUTION IN CORNWALL

The Queen of Spain Fritillary is a very rare immigrant which is seen only in a few, mainly coastal, tetrads, although it has been claimed that more have been seen in Cornwall than in any other county (Emmet and Heath 1990). In the great migration year of 1945, twenty-five were recorded in a valley near Portreath in September, all in first-class condition; it has been suggested that these were the progeny of an earlier immigrant female (Penhallurick 1996), which had succeeded in breeding here, but if this was so, no adults were seen flying in the following year, implying that no stages had survived the ensuing winter; certainly mating and egg-laying have been observed elsewhere in Britain. Another specimen was seen near Bude in July of the same year.

Other sightings have been in August 1947 at Lamorran Woods; an unconfirmed report at Daymer Bay in August 1973, and most recently at Lansallos Cove in June 1998.

HABITAT AND ECOLOGY

Little is known about the habitat requirements in Britain of this essentially European butterfly, but as with all sun-loving species, hot and dry combes, valleys, heathlands and dunes are probably the most favoured sites. It has however been seen visiting an urban flower garden outside the county, so it may appear almost anywhere.

The Queen of Spain Fritillary has several generations in its homelands, and overwintering apparently can occur in almost any stage of development. It is most likely to be seen in Cornwall during the late summer months, although earlier sightings are not impossible.

CAUSES OF DECLINE OR INCREASE

As with most immigrants, the causes for its presence or absence in any year depend on the weather and temperature systems of the continent, and also on a suitable wind at the correct time to bring it across the Channel.

LARVAL FOODPLANTS

The specimens believed to have bred near Portreath showed an interest in Common-Dog Violet (*Viola riviniana*), but were not seen to lay eggs; other species of violet may also be used. But the main foodplant in northern Europe seems to be the Field Pansy (*Viola arvensis*), which is common in arable fields in Cornwall, or Wild Pansy (*Viola tricolor*), which occurs mostly as a garden weed.

High Brown Fritillary *Argynnis adippe*

NYMPHALIDAE

No. of tetrads (1995–2000): 3
Status in Cornwall: resident
Regional priority: high
Regional rate of change: decreasing, -13%

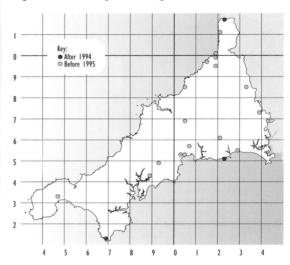

Key:
● After 1994
○ Before 1995

DISTRIBUTION IN CORNWALL

Since 1906, only 14 sites for the High Brown Fritillary have been recognised in Cornwall (Smith, F.H.N. 1997), of which nine were probably breeding sites, with another four casual nectaring stations; at only one does the butterfly now breed.

Since 1990, it has been recorded at only five sites. It is still present at the Welcombe and Marsland nature reserve, but it is probably extinct elsewhere in Cornwall. The habitat at Backways Cove is probably still suitable, with abundant larval foodplants on south facing, bracken-covered slopes. It is, however, unlikely now to be present at the other post-1990 sites, such as Boscundle, Calstock and Kynance Cove, all of which were probably only nectaring stations and not breeding sites. The butterflies seen at Kynance in 1957 and 1996 may have come from nearby, or possibly from Godolphin, Tregonning or even further afield. The records from Boscundle in 1976 and 1992 indicate a breeding colony in the vicinity, but no suitable habitat has been found there, despite extensive searches. Colonies may occur in the upper Luxulyan valley, or in the Fal valley between St Michael Penkevil and Grampound. The single record from Calstock is likely to be a wanderer from Devon. Suitable habitat remains at Higher Crankan, near Penzance, but there are no records since 1973 (Simpson 1974).

The scarcity of records of the High Brown Fritillary in Cornwall may be partly due to confusion with the Dark Green Fritillary. Large brown fritillaries, seen outside woodland or on the coast, are generally assumed to be the latter, although four High Brown Fritillary records in the county (two at Kynance, one each at Talland and Backways Cove) have been from non-wooded, coastal sites. It is therefore possible that the butterfly could have been more common in Cornwall than was realised.

HABITAT AND ECOLOGY

The habitat requirements of this species are extremely specific, and it is now generally accepted that warm bracken-covered slopes with abundant violets and always close to woodland are the most suitable. The larvae require exceptionally warm vegetation and in most habitats bask on dead bracken, which reaches high temperatures in spring sunshine (Warren 1995). Warren and Oates (1995) suggest that the key vegetational requirements for the larvae of the High Brown Fritillary are as follows: 1) bracken fronds which are from 40–110cm tall; 2) bracken density of 10–30 fronds per square metre; 3) a canopy between 30–70%; 4) violets making up 10–25% of the vegetation; 5) dead bracken for egg-laying should represent about 60% of the ground cover; 6) residual grass cover of 20–30%

The presence of Sheep's Sorrel (*Rumex acetosella*) usually indicates that the soil is too acid to support violets (Matthew Oates, *pers. comm.*). The ecology of the High Brown Fritillary is detailed in the national Species Action Plan (Barnett and Warren 1995), and in the Millennium Atlas (Asher *et al.* 2001).

The nature reserve at Welcombe and Marsland is now being successfully managed for the High Brown Fritillary by cutting small areas of European gorse (*Ulex europaeus*) on a 10–15 year cycle, followed by raking up of dead vegetation; there is a flush of violets after cutting. Cutting height is carefully controlled to allow some plants to be left uncut for shelter. Bracken is allowed to encroach into the areas cleared of gorse, but pathways and small glades are made once or twice in the growing season, or in late summer, followed by another cut in the following winter. Consequently, a fresh crop of violets appears before gorse and bracken re-grow and begin to shade out low growing plants.

This type of habitat can also be maintained by cattle and pony grazing, which breaks up the litter sufficiently to give good densities of foodplant.

Adults are most often seen in July, although there are occasional records from early June and late August (Penhallurick 1996); 1997 was an early season with emergences in late May in Devon (Matthew Oates, *pers. comm.*).

CAUSES OF DECLINE OR INCREASE

The High Brown Fritillary once occurred in woodland at Barteliver Wood, Coombe Valley, Dunmere, Herodsfoot, Keveral, Lamorran and Luckett. Many of these woods are now unsuitable owing to the excessive planting of conifers and to a reduction in coppicing. The butterfly may have been lost from all but one of these sites owing to tree growth creating too much shade; but it still could occur in the vicinity of Barteliver and Lamorran Woods in the Fal valley.

The species still survives at Welcombe and Marsland nature reserve because, as detailed above, the south-facing, bracken-covered slope is specifically managed for fritillaries. Of the nine other probable post-1990 breeding sites, only Backways Cove and Higher Crankan may still be suitable; both have bracken-covered hillside, but both would require sympathetic management. Cessation of grazing on these hillsides, as at Higher Crankan, may be one of the causes of decline.

CONSERVATION

The national Species Action Plan for this butterfly (Barnett and Warren 1995) highlights twenty-eight actions of low, medium or high priority. Action 24, low priority, is to survey sites for potential re-introduction within the former range and to encourage the restoration of suitable breeding habitats.

Action 10, high priority, calls for the implementation of appropriate management in the vicinity of former colonies, in the hope that favourable habitats can be re-created. Five sites meet this criteria: Backways Cove, Cancleave, Higher Crankan, Kilkhampton Common and Seaton Valley. Action 11, low priority, calls for appropriate management on new sites within the former range, and two fall into this category: St Cleer Common and Tuckingmill. Action 14, also low priority, calls for strategically-placed re-introductions into networks of suitable habitats; two sites meet this criteria at Backways Cove and Higher Crankan. Re-introduction into former woodlands at Barteliver and Lamorran Woods and at Luckett could also be considered; the latter is already managed for the Heath Fritillary (p. 101).

The local Species Action Plan (Cornwall Biodiversity Initiative 1998) calls for the establishment of a captive-bred population using stock from Cornwall and/or Devon, and the subsequent re-introduction of the High Brown Fritillary to at least two sites, following restoration of the habitat.

Some of the north Cornwall sites were surveyed in 1992 (Clarke and Grove 1992), as part of an extensive exploration in Devon and Exmoor. A more detailed study of historic and potential sites in Cornwall was made in 1997–98 (Spalding 1998).

Released captive-bred specimen at Cabilla Woods, 2001.

Following this last survey, and under licence from English Nature, in consultation with the Devon Wildlife Trust and Dartmoor National Park, a single female, fortunately fertilised, was captured in 1999 at Aish Tor, Dartmoor, for the Cornwall Branch of Butterfly Conservation, to enable a captive breeding programme to be set up (Hoskin 2000).

The female laid between 50–100 eggs, which resulted, in the following year, in the emergence of 76 adult butterflies. It was intended to collect fresh stock in 2000, but unfortunately it did not prove possible, so the captive specimens were then allowed to breed with themselves. The early part of the year 2001 was subject to the restrictions imposed by foot-and-mouth disease, when it was considered unlikely that entry into Dartmoor would be allowed in time for fresh stock to be captured. Consequently it was agreed to terminate this breeding programme for the time being and release the captive butterflies into the wild at an appropriate site.

The site at Cabilla Woods, between Bodmin and Liskeard, had been prepared as a secure release site by the Cornwall Wildlife Trust and, on 19 July 2001, 17 females and three males were released; butterflies were reported for several days afterwards. It remains to be seen if any progeny survive into 2002. This programme, completed under licence from English Nature has nevertheless increased knowledge about captive rearing, site suitability and management priorities in Cornwall.

LARVAL FOODPLANTS

Common Dog-violet (*Viola riviniana*) is a known larval foodplant in Cornwall, but Pale Dog-violet (*Viola lactea*) which, although nationally scarce, is found on some drier heaths in the county, could be a possible alternative.

ABERRATIONS

Aberrations in this species are not common, but none have yet been recorded in Cornwall.

Table 3. Records of High Brown Fritillary in Cornwall since 1906.

Site name	Year recorded	Possible breeding sites
Backways Cove	1993	Yes?
Barteliver Wood	1972	Yes?
Boscundle	1976, 1992	No
Calstock	1991	No
Coombe Valley	1974	Yes
Dunmere Wood	1951–52	Yes
Herodsfoot	1910	Yes
Higher Crankan	1973	Yes
Keveral Wood	1974, 1989	Yes
Kynance	1957, 1996	Yes
Lamorran Wood	1958	Yes
Luckett	1969	Yes
Marsland	1992–97	Yes
Talland Bay	1997	No

Dark Green Fritillary *Argynnis aglaja*

No. of tetrads (1995–2000): 49
Status in Cornwall: resident
Regional priority: low
Regional rate of change: increasing, +25%

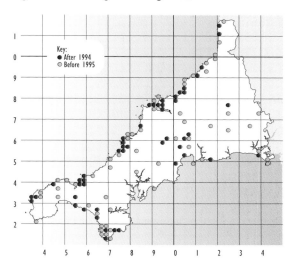

Key:
● After 1994
○ Before 1995

DISTRIBUTION IN CORNWALL

This species, while the most common fritillary in the county, is locally widespread. There are only five full 10km squares where it has never been recorded, and four of those cover the higher parts of Bodmin Moor. However, its stronghold has always been the coastal regions, especially the north coast, and inland colonies are rarer and more isolated. The distribution map tends to show that it is less common in south-east Cornwall; in contrast there are now few sites with suitable habitats in the county west of Camborne, where the butterfly cannot be expected to occur. It has even been seen on a garden buddleja in Carbis Bay. It is probably commonest on the dune systems of the north coast: at the Towans east of Hayle, at the Perransands complex and round the Camel estuary, and many dozens, if not hundreds, can be seen at these sites during the flight season. There has possibly been something of a decline in numbers in recent years at some of the inland sites, such as Breney Common and Treskilling Downs, and perhaps there has also been some under-recording, but overall its status in the county appears quite healthy.

Fortunately, there can be little confusion with the Silver-washed Fritillary (p. 97), since there is little or no overlap in territory, although their flight periods are much the same. There could be confusion with the High Brown Fritillary (p. 92) if the latter had a wider distribution; but it is always worth checking every Dark Green Fritillary, just on the off-chance that it may be a High Brown Fritillary.

HABITAT AND ECOLOGY

The Dark Green Fritillary enjoys more exposed habitats than any other fritillary. Typically it is to be found on large, windswept dunes and moorland of the Cornish coast; very few are reported from open woodland. Apart from the dunes, the coastal slopes embrace heaths and flower-rich grasslands with occasional scrub and bracken. It prefers relatively short swards up to 15–20cm high, so that light grazing and the occasional burning does it no real harm. Indeed at Rinsey and also at Botallack after the extensive fires in the hot, dry summer of 1995, the butterfly appeared again with renewed strength in subsequent years.

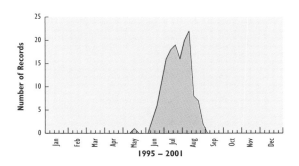

1995 – 2001

It is said to occupy discrete colonies, although the adults are highly mobile, strong fliers, and they tend to occur at low densities over large areas. The butterflies are attracted to purple flowers such as thistles (*Cirsium* spp.), teasels (*Dipsacus* spp.) and particularly to Red Valerian (*Centranthus ruber*). An observation at Upton Towans at the end of July 1999 showed over 50 butterflies feasting on a patch of the latter, no more than 20m by 2m in size; none were seen anywhere else on the Towans that day, and the Valerian must have attracted the entire population. The flight period nationally is normally considered as mid-June to mid-August, but in Cornwall in warm years, specimens can emerge in mid-May and it can still be on the wing in late August. One seen in late September, in good condition, gives a hint of a partial second brood. But the peak period is undoubtedly mid-to late July.

CAUSES OF DECLINE OR INCREASE

The national decline of the Dark Green Fritillary, which began at the beginning of the last century and accelerated from the 1950s, certainly affected the Cornish colonies. Now, however, this decline appears to have been reversed, and, indeed, increases are again being recorded (Spalding with Bourn 2000). However the extent to which this has occurred is controversial; some have claimed that the last 15 years has seen both a contraction of the butterfly's range in Cornwall and a reduction in numbers at the small inland colonies.

Decline, where it has taken place, is usually due to overgrazing, mainly by rabbits which eat the foodplants, or to destruction of habitat by the improvement of grassland, or by development.

CONSERVATION

Preservation of rough coastal dunes and heathlands, mostly in their present state with moderate rabbit grazing would seem to be the main requirement; fortunately much of this land is now in the hands of the National Trust or other bodies. Requests to their tenant farmers not to plough too close to cliff-top edges would create corridors along which the species could spread. Part of the Welcombe and Marsland nature reserve is now managed for this butterfly.

LARVAL FOODPLANTS

Common Dog-violet (*Viola riviniana*) seems to be the most acceptable; other violet species may prove attractive, such as Marsh Violet (*Viola palustris* ssp. *juressi*), or the rare Hairy Violet (*Viola hirta*), which is found on some of the north coast dunes, but their use has not been confirmed in Cornwall.

ABERRATIONS

Females in Cornwall are often of a dusky hue, being suffused with black and green scaling, and resemble the subspecies *scotica*; this form may be seen most frequently on the north coast dunes. One has been recorded in which only the right forewing was so coloured. A partial ab. *albescens* was reported from Porthgwarra in 1978, in which the tawny ground colour was replaced by creamy-white.

Silver-washed Fritillary *Argynnis paphia*

No. of tetrads (1995–2000): 81
Status in Cornwall: resident
Regional priority: medium
Regional rate of change: increasing, +12%

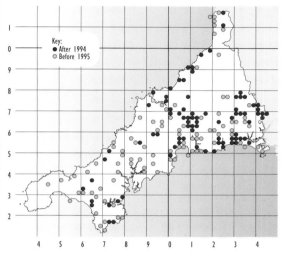

Key:
● After 1994
○ Before 1995

DISTRIBUTION IN CORNWALL

The Silver-washed Fritillary is the largest and most spectacular fritillary to occur in Cornwall, and good numbers can still be seen in suitable woods and nearby lanes and hedgerows, although the frequency tends to diminish towards the west of the county, mainly due to the lack of suitable habitat. Extensive searches in the few woodlands in Penwith have revealed no sites, although at one time or another it has been recorded in almost every 10km square in Cornwall. Recent recordings have been made at Trevarno and Godolphin Woods, which at present are the most westerly sites in the county. In the Lizard peninsula it still survives in the Gwendreath valley, behind the nearby Kennack Sands, and at Bochym; it has been seen at these sites as recently as 2000–01. But the main concentration of colonies undoubtedly lies in the woods that flank the upper lengths of the river Fowey and its tributaries, mainly south-east of Bodmin, and also in the woods in the valleys north of St Austell. A scatter of colonies inhabits the woods north of Seaton and they also occur in the wooded areas around the river valleys west of the Tamar. Another group of colonies can be found in similar situations near the north coast between Rock and Millook, and in the upper reaches of the river Camel; the Marsland nature reserve is partly managed for this butterfly. Surprisingly there are no recent records from the woods in the Fal valley, despite it being seen there before 1995.

HABITAT AND ECOLOGY

The Silver-washed Fritillary is essentially a butterfly of woodland, preferably oak, and can tolerate more shaded conditions than other fritillaries, providing there are sufficient open spaces for sunlight and warmth to penetrate, so as to stimulate the growth of the larval foodplant. It can also be found in lanes, hedges and banks close to woodland. The butterfly is most frequently found nectaring on brambles and thistles in clearings and along rides. The male in particular has a strong, gliding flight when patrolling its territory and while awaiting a passing female, a habit which makes identification easier. The female is dimorphic: in form *valezina* the tawny ground colour is replaced

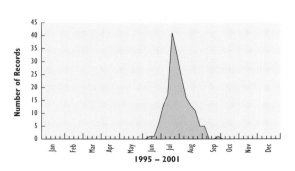

1995 – 2001

by a beautiful greeny-bronze. This form is common in the New Forest but rare in Cornwall.

The Silver-washed Fritillary is single-brooded, emerging in early July, although specimens have been seen in mid-June in Cornwall. The flight period normally lasts until late August; adults have been seen in September and rarely even in early October.

CAUSES OF DECLINE OR INCREASE

The principal cause of any decline is change in woodland management, often leading to increased shade and the reduction in density of the larval foodplants; but in central and eastern Cornwall, the species seems to be holding its own (Spalding with Bourn 2000).

CONSERVATION

Part of the Welcombe and Marsland nature reserve is managed for this species; otherwise there are no woodlands in Cornwall

Silver-washed Fritillary f. *valezina*.

which are specifically maintained for this butterfly. It is essential that clearings and rides should be kept free of overshadowing top canopy, and scrub should be periodically cleared to encourage the growth of larval foodplants.

LARVAL FOODPLANTS

Common Dog-violet (*Viola riviniana*) is the preferred foodplant; the full range of other violet species is not known (Emmet and Heath 1990).

The butterfly does not lay its eggs on the foodplant, but on a nearby tree, at a height of 1–2m above the ground; the mossy side of the trunk, or a low branch, is chosen as the most desirable place.

ABERRATIONS

The greeny-bronze dimorphic form of the female, f. *valezina*, has been recorded twice in Cornwall, once near Seaton in September 1986 and another in 1966 in a small glade in a densely wooded area in the Lizard Peninsula.

A partial form also exists, where only the hindwings have the greeny-bronze colour; one was seen in 1964. Other aberrations exist, mainly involving varying degrees of melanism, but none have been recorded in Cornwall.

Marsh Fritillary *Euphydryas (Eurodryas) aurinia*

No. of tetrads (1995–2000): 30
Status in Cornwall: resident
Regional priority: high
Regional rate of change: increasing, +27%

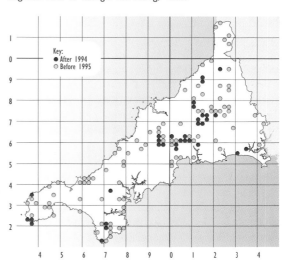

Key:
● After 1994
○ Before 1995

DISTRIBUTION IN CORNWALL

The Marsh Fritillary is a declining species and the south-west now contains about one fifth of the total national population, of which a small proportion still survive in Cornwall; but even here they are at risk. Penhallurick (1996) lists many sites known to have harboured this butterfly in the 1950s, but only three now have colonies. With new discoveries, the figure expanded to 26 by 1990, although in 2000 only eight remained, despite a further 22 new colonies being located in this decade alone; four of them had been lost by the time that 18 were resurveyed in 1999/2000. Of the survivors, two have been classified as large, on a count of larval webs, which is more accurate than counting adults in assessing the strength of a colony; both of these sites, at Goss Moor and Breney Common, had over 100 webs. Both cover extensive areas of land and are nationally important for the Marsh Fritillary; the former is being managed by English Nature, with the latter owned and managed by the Cornwall Wildlife Trust.

One site, at Colvannick Marsh is classified as medium with ten-plus webs, while the rest are considered small with less than ten webs, or an adult population of about 50 (Hobson *et al.* 2001).

There still remain some small coastal colonies in west Penwith, notably in the area of Gwennap Head, with another at Bochym in the Lizard which is in the care of English Nature. A third exists near Stithians reservoir.

A number of colonies have disappeared from north Cornwall in the last ten years, and only a handful now remain there. South-east Cornwall, never a favoured area, has fared even worse, and there is now only one site near Polbathic, where the butterfly appears to maintain a tenuous hold.

The Marsh Fritillary is still found at low density in suitable habitats to the south and west of Bodmin Moor, and further populations may await discovery there. The medium-sized colony at Colvannick Marsh has a cluster of smaller sites to its east.

HABITAT AND ECOLOGY

The Marsh Fritillary inhabits open, grassy areas in damp, unimproved meadows and heaths, particularly where the grass grows in tussocks, and where there is ample larval foodplant in between them. For the latter to flourish, the sward length needs

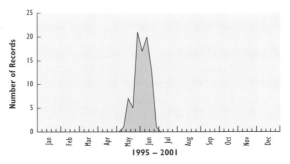

1995 – 2001

not to be too rank, nor too short, with an average height of between 5–25cm. These habitats are often situated on west- or south-facing slopes.

The larvae of this species in its early stages are gregarious and spin protective webs, which can readily be seen in the early autumn. As already mentioned, a count of the larval webs at this time of the year can often give a better measure of a colony's strength, than the counting of adult butterflies.

Recent research has also shown that the Marsh Fritillary survives in what are termed metapopulations. These contain smaller, distinct colonies, which are self-contained, but from which, in warm summers, females will sometimes disperse to re-colonise vacant areas or to establish new colonies, if suitable habitats can be found. Small colonies are prone to extinction, due to adverse weather, changes in the habitat such as over-growth of vegetation, or infestation by parasitic wasps of the genus *Cotesia*; but as long as there are other colonies not too far away, re-colonisation can take place later. The distance, though, that females can disperse is limited, so that sites that lose their colonies will not naturally be re-colonised if the nearest survivor is more than 15km away.

For a metapopulation to survive, the colonisation rate in the region must be at least equal to the rate of extinction. The larger the area covered by a metapopulation, the greater is its potential chance of survival.

The butterfly is single-brooded and can be seen on the wing most abundantly in May and June, although July is not uncommon.

CAUSES OF DECLINE OR INCREASE

Drainage of wetlands, ploughing of fields, fertilising meadows and overgrazing have all contributed to the decline of this species. In Britain, as in much of Europe, it is no longer profitable for farmers to support light-grazing regimes, so grasslands are either over-grazed, often with the improvement of fertilisers, to the extent that the larval foodplant can no longer support colonies, or they are simply abandoned and left to become overgrown with scrub. One site in the east of the county was recently converted to flax growing (Spalding with Bourn 2000).

Many of the remaining pockets of suitable habitat are now so small and fragmented that the chances of the Marsh Fritillary's long-term survival in them is very slight.

CONSERVATION

Any conservation must be aimed at the maintenance of habitats, preferably on a scale that can continue to support metapopulations; this can be best achieved by management agreements with land owners.

A prerequisite, though, is the identification of colonies, and other areas where suitable habitats either exist or could be created. Extensive searches have already been made on parts of Bodmin Moor in the autumn of 2000. Twenty sites were considered to be overgrazed, while a further nine were undergrazed and supported too much rush (*Juncus* spp.). Some of the sites were thought to be too wet or too exposed, but many of those which were overgrazed could be reclaimed as potential habitats for the butterfly, if light grazing regimes were instituted at some future date (Hobson and Budd 2001).

Similarly, a number of sites in west Cornwall and the Lizard, which once held colonies, have been visited in the last five years; most would be suitable for reclamation.

LARVAL FOODPLANTS

The larvae feed almost exclusively on Devil's-bit Scabious (*Succisa pratensis*) which is widespread in most of Cornwall, although it is much more sporadic along the south coast, which perhaps explains the rarity of the butterfly there. On Cornish sites strong large plants are chosen, usually growing in turf that is 12–25cm tall (Hobson *et al.* 2001). The butterfly has been known to use Field Scabious (*Knautia arvensis*).

ABERRATIONS

The Marsh Fritillary has several subspecies. The English downland form is named f. *anglicana*, but whether the Cornish populations are of this form is not certain; both Scotland and Ireland are said to have their own forms (Emmet and Heath 1990).

Apart from geographical localities, the butterfly is also a variable species, but so far only one unnamed aberration has been recorded in Cornwall, at Breney Common in 1999. In this, much of the orange on the upper forewings was replaced by pale fawn.

Heath Fritillary *Melitaea (Mellicta) athalia*

No. of tetrads (1995–2000): 2
Status in Cornwall: resident
Regional priority: high
Regional rate of change: stable, 0%

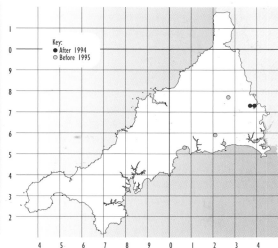

Key:
● After 1994
○ Before 1995

DISTRIBUTION IN CORNWALL

The Heath Fritillary is now restricted to a small area of south-east Cornwall near Luckett, close to the Devon border, where annual populations probably exceed hundreds; the habitat is specifically managed as a nature reserve on behalf of the Duchy of Cornwall. In the last decade, another colony also on Duchy land has been discovered only a short distance west of Luckett, at Deer Park Wood, Broadgate. Formerly a colony also existed at nearby Stoke Climsland, but no butterflies have recently been recorded there. Although one of the rarest resident British butterflies, high numbers can be expected to emerge, at least in hot summers, at these two localities near the village of Luckett.

A small colony was known in 1964 in the Looe valley, but unfortunately the site was bulldozed out of existence. There seems no possibility that the butterfly exists anywhere else in the county, but expansion may yet occur around its known habitats.

HABITAT AND ECOLOGY

The species lives only in very warm micro-climates, such as are provided by the deep valleys of the Tamar and its tributaries. It lives in discrete colonies, which, nevertheless, can contain high populations. Ideally, the warm, sunny habitat should be well-drained, with low vegetation, and plentiful larval foodplants in an otherwise sparse ground flora. The colonies are moderately mobile, so adjacent new woodland clearings can be taken over when existing ones are being shaded out. It is tolerant of bracken, which is widespread at Deer Park, and the dead fronds of the previous season may afford shelter for the overwintering larvae.

The flight period normally runs from early June to the middle of July, although specimens in Cornwall have been seen in late May. There is no second brood.

CAUSES OF DECLINE OR INCREASE

The species requires both shelter from wind and rain, and a sunny microclimate; consequently its relative abundance is dependent on the temperatures in spring and summer and the

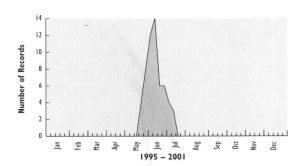

hours of sunshine. It is probably these requirements which prevent the species from leaving the valleys, where it is resident, to move to others, many of which must hold several of its varied larval foodplants. High numbers of adults emerge in warm or hot springs and summers, but far fewer in damp, cool ones. The butterfly also migrates short distances to newly-opened, sheltered and warm areas of the same valley, where recent tree-felling has occurred, so it will not always be found in exactly the same places as before.

CONSERVATION

Fortunately, the few areas where the butterfly now resides are being managed specifically for it by the Duchy of Cornwall, with advice from English Nature and Butterfly Conservation. The sites

Heath Fritillary site at Deer Park Wood.

are regularly monitored. There is a suggestion that there should be a re-introduction at the former colony site at Herodsfoot (Spalding with Bourn 2000), after suitable management has taken place.

LARVAL FOODPLANTS

Common Cow-wheat (*Melampyrum pratense* ssp. *pratense*) appears to be the favoured foodplant in Kent, where one of the other main reservoirs of the Heath Fritillary still survives, although this foodplant is not popular with the Cornish species; indeed the plant is only local in the county, but occurs near Luckett. The Heath Fritillary in Cornwall seems to prefer Ribwort Plantain (*Plantago lanceolata*), although alternatives are not uncommon: Foxglove (*Digitalis purpurea*), Germander Speedwell (*Veronica chamaedrys*), Ivy-leaved Speedwell (*Veronica hederifolia*), Yarrow (*Achillea millefolium*), Lesser Celandine (*Ranunculus ficaria*) and Wood Sage (*Teucrium scorodonia*) have all been recorded, and others may yet be discovered.

ABERRATIONS

Aberrations are not uncommon in this species, and a number have been taken or recorded. Ab. *cymothoe*, in its extreme almost completely melanic form, was seen at Luckett in 1994, together with a less extreme example. Another had been photographed previously in 1962 (Smith, F.H.N. 1997). Other aberrations, all seen in the Luckett region were: ab. *tetramelana*, ab. *corythallia*, ab. *eos*, ab. *melanoleuca*, ab. *obsoleta* and ab. *latonigena*; there have also been a number of unnamed aberrations.

Left: male ab. of Heath Fritillary, Luckett, East Cornwall, 1996. Right: extreme ab. *cymothoe*, June 1994.

Speckled Wood *Pararge aegeria*

No. of tetrads (1995–2000): 467
Status in Cornwall: resident
Regional priority: none
Regional rate of change: increasing, +14%

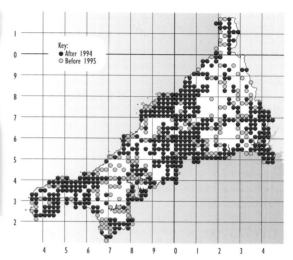

Key:
● After 1994
○ Before 1995

DISTRIBUTION IN CORNWALL

The Speckled Wood is found throughout Cornwall, having been recorded in every 10km square. It has greatly expanded its range in Britain over the last few decades, although some new colonies in northern England are due to releases; otherwise the increase may be due to the greater availability of shady woodland. This expansion followed a marked decline in the early part of the last century, although the south-west has always been the main reservoir, possibly because the butterfly's habitat requirements are slightly different here.

HABITAT AND ECOLOGY

The butterfly is unique in Britain in being able to spend the winter in either the larval stage or as a pupa. Since though the caterpillars continue to feed whenever the temperature is high enough in the shorter months, the pupal stage represents true hibernation. Caterpillars at the fourth moult, or slightly earlier, can over-winter successfully; younger ones are usually killed by any severe weather. But some develop more rapidly and pupate, depending on temperature and exposure to light, in which stage they also pass the winter. These latter are usually the first to emerge in the following spring, often as early as February, to be followed slightly later by those that over-wintered as caterpillars; there is often an overlap. Thereafter hardly a week passes without a Speckled Wood appearing somewhere in Cornwall. But it is possible to distinguish three main peaks of emergence by the numbers on the wing at any one time: from March to early May; late May to early July and late July to September. Fresh specimens seen in October and November may, in good weather, be products of a partial fourth brood, although in the appalling autumn of 2000 there was little indication of even a third brood. The Speckled Wood is one of a handful of Cornish butterflies that have been recorded in every month of the year (Penhallurick 1996).

The adult butterfly is normally associated with sun-dappled woodland fringes, rides and glades, but in Cornwall, while not forsaking these haunts, it has extended its range to become a

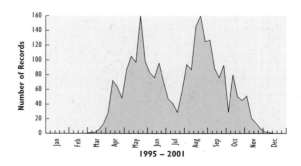

butterfly of hedges and shady lanes, railway embankments and even gardens. Indeed one has been seen flying down Causewayhead in the centre of Penzance, where it paused to investigate some foliage outside a florist's shop.

It is also one of the earliest and latest fliers in the day and it has been seen before sunrise and is often flying after sunset, providing the weather is warm.

The butterfly is represented in Cornwall by ssp. *tircis*, which is said to be different from those found on the Isles of Scilly, ssp. *insula* (p. 125). They appear to differ in the colour and size of the pale patches on the wings.

CAUSES OF DECLINE OR INCREASE

Like all common butterflies, this species suffers periodic fluctuations, usually due to poor weather, but it seems to have no difficulty re-establishing itself once the weather becomes more benign. A period of unseasonable weather can though affect individual broods. But there is no sign of any real decrease in Cornwall.

CONSERVATION

No specific conservation is required for this butterfly.

LARVAL FOODPLANTS

While catholic in its choice of grasses, and over fifteen have been recorded, the larvae tend to prefer False Brome (*Brachypodium sylvaticum*), Cock's-foot (*Dactylis glomerata*), Yorkshire-fog (*Holcus lanatus*) and Common-couch (*Elytrigia repens*). Apparently it is not so much the species of grass that matters, but its position in sun or shade.

ABERRATIONS

A number of aberrations have been recorded, some from Cornwall; most are associated with the colour, size and spacings of the creamy-white markings. Ab. *saturatior*, where these markings are almost completely obscured by blackish scaling, has been seen at Park Shady in May 1948 and in the Isles of Scilly. Apparently in the Scillonian ssp. *insula*, the creamy spots are a deeper yellowish-orange and more nearly resemble the nominate species from southern Europe.

Wall *Lasiommata megera*

No. of tetrads (1995–2000): 190
Status in Cornwall: resident
Regional priority: low
Regional rate of change: slight increase, +7%

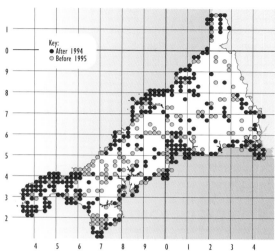

Key:
● After 1994
◐ Before 1995

DISTRIBUTION IN CORNWALL

The Wall, or Wall Brown as it is sometimes called, is widely distributed in Cornwall, and at one time or another has been recorded in every 10km square, although there is an area around St Columb Major where no records have been made since 1994. However, since 1995 it has become slightly more frequent in the western part of the county, with a concentration towards west Penwith. Yet there is also a large group of sightings in the St Austell region. Apart from these two areas, the butterfly seems inclined to favour a near coastal habitat. Whether this represents the real distribution of the butterfly, or is due to a greater concentration of observers near the coast remains in doubt. Certainly the species has become more numerous in west Cornwall in the last few years, especially since 1980, reaching a peak in 1999, when most sites visited there, at appropriate times, never failed to produce one or two specimens.

The butterfly is liable to large annual fluctuations in abundance, but it appears to be more stable on monitored transects in Cornwall than nationally.

HABITAT AND ECOLOGY

The Wall may be encountered almost anywhere, except in shady woodland. Essentially it is a sun-loving butterfly and favours hedges, particularly Cornish hedges, where it delights to sun itself on any exposed stonework; rough, unimproved grassland; old industrial sites, with plenty of bare ground; bridleways and gardens, where it will sit with its wings open to gain reflected warmth. Equally desirable are fences and walls – hence its name.

Adults first emerge in May and June, although appearances in Cornwall in March and April are not uncommon. These breed quickly to produce a second generation in July and August, sometimes prolonged into September. Especially in warm periods, and almost without fail in Cornwall, (although the wet autumn of 2000 was an exception) a small proportion of the second brood produce a partial third brood from September to October, or even November. What is not known is the stage at which the eggs or larvae of this late brood spend the winter. Nor

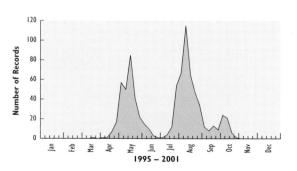

1995 – 2001

for that matter is it entirely certain at what stage those insects, which do not produce a third brood, hibernate. Frohawk (1934) implies that some, which do not emerge as adults in the autumn, nevertheless pupate to over-winter, while the remainder stay as larvae, possibly resembling the Speckled Wood (p. 103); much apparently depends on the temperature.

CAUSES OF DECLINE OR INCREASE

It could be argued that the Wall has retreated in recent years to the coastal regions in Cornwall, a retreat presumably caused by agricultural improvements inland. Yet this cannot be the full explanation. The area south-east of Hayle is one of the most extensively farmed areas in the county, where almost all the fields are cultivated and often as many as four crops are taken from them in a year, and where such grassland as has survived has undoubtedly been improved. But even in this 'desert' the Wall not only manages to hold its own, but also, up to 1999, has actually increased in numbers; unfortunately the terrible weather in 2000–01 caused something of a reverse, but it should be noted that it was not due solely to agriculture. The answer probably lies in the extensive network of footpaths, bridleways, unmetalled farmtracks and country lanes, which frequently bound or bisect the fields, so providing, not only favourable habitats, but also lines of communication by which the butterfly can move about. It can fly considerable distances and has even been seen 50km out at sea off the Norfolk coast. Cornwall is criss-crossed by large numbers of footpaths and tracks, which are a lifeline, not only for the Wall, but for several other species as well.

CONSERVATION

The maintenance and extension of the Cornish system of footpaths and bridleways is important for this species, as for others.

LARVAL FOODPLANTS

A variety of grasses are chosen and eight are listed by most authorities, among which are: Cock's-foot (*Dactylis glomerata*), Wavy Hair-grass (*Deschampsia flexuosa*) which is mainly confined to Bodmin Moor, Common Bent (*Agrostis tenuis*), Black Bent (*Agrostis gigantea*) which is scarce and is mostly found in arable fields in east Cornwall, Yorkshire-fog (*Holcus lanatus*), Annual Meadow-grass (*Poa annua*) and False Brome (*Brachypodium sylvaticum*) which is, however, absent from the main granite areas.

ABERRATIONS

A number of rare aberrations are known, which usually involve the ground colour of the wings or the extent of the black markings. A specimen ab. *medeolugens*, in which the whole central space of the forewings is black, was captured near Penzance in August 1920, and another was taken in west Cornwall in August 1950.

Wall ab., Trewavas Head, west Cornwall.

Marbled White *Melanargia galathea*

No. of tetrads (1995–2000): 51
Status in Cornwall: resident
Regional priority: medium
Regional rate of change: increasing, +48%

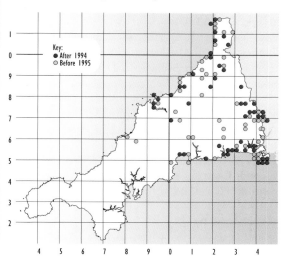

Key:
● After 1994
○ Before 1995

DISTRIBUTION IN CORNWALL

The Marbled White is confined to the east of the county, with few records west of the rivers Camel and Fowey, where there are less than half-a-dozen records in the south and less than a score in the north. There is some evidence for believing that the butterfly appears to move west in hot, dry summers and that ephemeral colonies had once set up on the north coast west of Padstow; they appeared at St Merryn and Constantine in the 1960s and 1970s, and more recently in 1979 at Sladesbridge, just east of Wadebridge. There have been several unconfirmed sightings in the 1980s and 1990s in the Ellenglaze Valley south of Newquay. On the south coast there have been no sightings west of Pentewan.

By far the most Cornish colonies of the Marbled White therefore lie in the area east of these rivers up to the Devon border. Small colonies exist along the coast from the Rock dunes to the Welcombe and Marsland nature reserve in the north, and also to a lesser extent inland. A slightly greater concentration lies in south-east Cornwall close to the upper reaches of the Tamar valley and in the coastal region west of Rame Head.

HABITAT AND ECOLOGY

The butterfly inhabits areas of unimproved grassland, with a tall sward, in coastal areas and on the culm measures of north Cornwall, but colonies can be very discrete, often only occupying one or two fields. It dislikes damp conditions, which may be the reason why it has not yet penetrated into west Cornwall; hence its preference for well-drained limestone and chalk regions in other areas. As with several other species, the adults are attracted to purple flowers, such as thistles (*Cirsium* spp.) and Knapweed (*Centaurea* spp.) for nectar.

The butterfly is single-brooded, and appears on the wing from mid-to late June, depending on the temperature, until mid-to late August, and has been seen rarely in September.

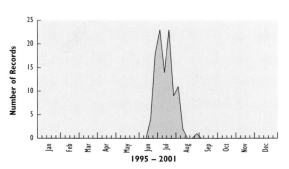

CAUSES OF DECLINE OR INCREASE

Destruction of habitat either by grassland improvement, over-grazing, too frequent cutting, or neglect causing scrub encroachment, are the principal causes for any decline. Fragmentation of habitat can also be a problem, as with most species, but fortunately the Marbled White is something of a traveller and there is always the possibility of new colonies being formed, or old ones being re-established. A series of hot dry summers may even lead to a temporary or permanent expansion in range.

CONSERVATION

Part of the Welcombe and Marsland nature reserve is managed for this species, otherwise there is little to be done except to ensure that long, uncut grassland remains unimproved. The acquisition of large areas of coastal grassland by the National Trust should improve the situation. Both over- and under-grazing should be resisted, as also the unnecessary cutting of roadside verges in the vicinity of colonies.

An attempted introduction of the Marbled White to an apparently suitable site near Lostwithiel in 1999, was successful for three or four years, but then did not survive a very wet winter.

LARVAL FOODPLANTS

Several grasses serve as foodplants but Red Fescue (*Festuca rubra*), which is common all over Cornwall, seems to be the most favoured. Alternatives are Sheep's-fescue (*Festuca ovina*), with a more restricted distribution in the county, Timothy (*Phleum pratense*), Cock's-foot (*Dactylis glomerata*), and possibly others.

ABERRATIONS

Although several major, but rare, aberrations occur, none have been seen in Cornwall.

Grayling *Hipparchia semele*

No. of tetrads (1995–2000): 55
Status in Cornwall: resident
Regional priority: medium
Regional rate of change: declining, -7%

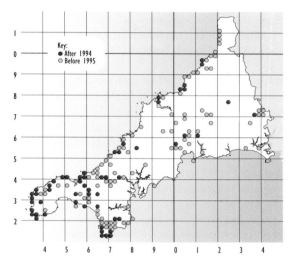

Key:
● After 1994
○ Before 1995

DISTRIBUTION IN CORNWALL

The Grayling is well-established in Cornwall, despite a reduction in the number of sites before 1995, but it now seems to have stabilised in its main strongholds; these are primarily in north and west Cornwall and the Lizard, where it tends to cling to the coast. It seems to be absent on the south coast from the Helford River to the Tamar, where it has never been strongly represented. It still occurs on several inland sites, most of which are again in the west, thinning out towards the east where few colonies survive. The butterfly seems to have declined most on the Lizard heaths, along the north coast, and in central Cornwall (Spalding 1995).

Good numbers can still be seen in several places in west Cornwall. On the coast, the stretch northwards from Gwennap Head to Land's End and again behind Wheal Cock and at Zennor Head, have prolific colonies.

Inland, occasional specimens may be seen near Drannock, Binner Downs and Penberthy, where they are associated with disused mines. On the north coast dunes they are widespread but it is unusual to see more than one or two at a time. It is currently recorded on three Cornish transects, on Gear Sands, Godolphin and Gwithian Towans.

HABITAT AND ECOLOGY

The adult butterflies occupy a wide variety of habitats, which must be dry and well-drained. They may be found on both maritime and inland grassland and heath, and also on the short turf of the dunes. In Cornwall they especially delight in abandoned industrial areas, such as old mines, quarries and railway tracks. But one essential factor is necessary on all sites: there must be plentiful areas of bare rock, stones and earth on which the butterflies can bask; they position themselves with their wings closed and then tilt them in such a way as to obtain the maximum benefit from the sun. When seen like this, they are almost invisible, owing to the excellent camouflage provided by the underside of the hindwings.

A remarkable occurrence was witnessed at Upton Towans on 14 August 1997. As already described, they are normally only seen here in ones and twos. On this day over 50 had congregated

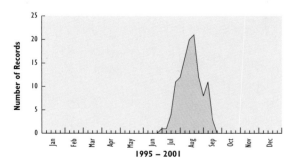

1995 – 2001

in an area of about 70m square. Many were engaged in courtship flights, while some had already entered into coition, and one was even seen egg-laying.

During the courtships, they often sat with their wings open, providing a rare opportunity to see the upper surfaces. It was a very hot day with 70% sun and only a moderate wind. Two days later, all but four had dispersed. Presumably they had originally gathered in order to mate.

Various subspecies inhabit some of the western extremeties of the British Isles, but not seemingly in Cornwall, where the nominate form *H. semele semele* is found.

There is only one brood a year and the adults emerge in Cornwall towards the end of June, peaking in July and early August, and lasting through until September, although specimens have been seen rarely in October.

CAUSES OF DECLINE OR INCREASE

As with most species, the chief threat to the Grayling is the destruction of habitat, whether by a lack of grazing leading to higher and denser vegetation and an absence of bare ground, or by the tidying-up of abandoned industrial sites, such as old mines, and the consequent loss of short turf and bare ground (Spalding and Haes 1995). The disappearance of the butterfly from much of the south coast may be partly due to scrub encroachment on the cliff slopes, with the resulting lack of bare ground.

CONSERVATION

Resistance to the reclamation of old mine sites is perhaps the most significant method of conservation in Cornwall, particularly inland, where sites are more at risk from advancing agriculture. There is also a danger that this process can be started by the removal of mine dumps for road building, as happened in the early 1980s, at Wheal Carpenter, when the Hayle by-pass was being constructed. Once the tips were removed the land was reclaimed for agriculture.

Management of coastal valleys in north Cornwall for the possible re-establishment of the Large Blue (p. 69) has increased the amount of suitable habitat for the Grayling, and these valleys now hold some of the strongest colonies in Cornwall.

LARVAL FOODPLANTS

The Grayling chiefly uses the finer grasses, such as Red Fescue (*Festuca rubra*) and, less common in Cornwall, Sheep's Fescue (*Festuca ovina*); alternatives are Bristle Bent (*Agrostis curtisii*) and Early Hair-grass (*Aira praecox*), both of which have a more restricted distribution in the county. Coarser species, such as Tufted Hair-grass (*Deschampsia cespitosa*), which is mainly confined to the north-east and centre of the county, and Marram Grass (*Ammophila arenaria*), only found on the sand dunes, are known to have been used occasionally.

ABERRATIONS

Aberrations are not uncommon in this species, and are mostly related to the prominent eye-spots on the upper-side of the forewing. Frohawk (1924) described a bred specimen from north Cornwall with two additional spots on each wing, ab. *quadrocellata*. Colour variation on the undersides of the hindwings is not uncommon, and ones with light patches have been observed in north Cornwall and near Truro.

Gatekeeper *Pyronia tithonus*

No. of tetrads (1995–2000): 407
Status in Cornwall: resident
Regional priority: none
Regional rate of change: increasing, +15%

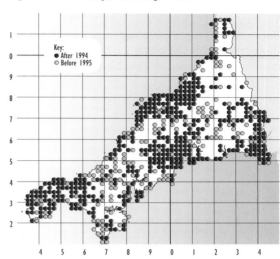

Key:
● After 1994
○ Before 1995

DISTRIBUTION IN CORNWALL

This butterfly is widespread all over the county, although it may have retreated slightly in the last decade from the higher moors; gaps in the distribution map probably represent an absence of recorders. In some years in July, it is the commonest species to be seen, except in the centres of urban areas.

HABITAT AND ECOLOGY

As the distribution map infers, the Gatekeeper can be seen in almost any habitat, so long as it contains nectar sources, of which bramble (*Rubus* spp.) is popular. But it mostly favours hedgerows (hence its alternative name of Hedge Brown) with lush growth at the base, and is therefore commoner on footpaths, bridleways and farm tracks, or on scrubland. It tends not to penetrate too deeply into woodland, but remains on the fringes.

The butterfly is single-brooded, appearing, in early years in mid-June; indeed one was even seen at Mullion in mid-May in 1988 and another at Botallack in early June 1996. But it normally appears early in July which is the peak month. The flight period extends to the second week of September, but specimens have been seen in late September and even early October in Cornwall.

CAUSES OF DECLINE OR INCREASE

Apart from annual fluctuations in numbers, to which all common butterflies are prone, there has probably been no overall decline in the species, and possibly even a slight increase. Short of proposals to flatten every Cornish hedge in the county, there is no perceived threat to the Gatekeeper.

CONSERVATION

No specific conservation methods are considered necessary for this species. It is, however, monitored along a number of Cornish transects.

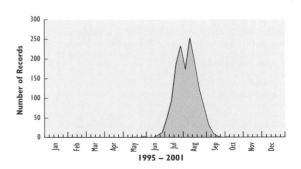

1995 – 2001

LARVAL FOODPLANTS

Various grasses are the common foodplant, but narrow-bladed species are preferred, such as the Fescues (*Festuca* spp.), of which Red Fescue (F. *rubra*) is the commonest in Cornwall, followed probably by Sheep's-Fescue (F. *ovina*). Meadow grasses (*Poa* spp.) and Common-couch (*Elytrigia repens*) are also used.

ABERRATIONS

There are several varieties of this species, in which one with extra spotting, ab. *excessa*, is apparently more common in Cornwall than in the south-east of the country (Penhallurick 1996) particularly around Godolphin (Smith, F.H.N. 1997). A very similar type of aberration, ab. *multi-ocellata* was seen at Pontsmill in 1994. A male of the pale yellowish-white form, ab. *subalbida* was captured by Frohawk in north Cornwall, after a female of this aberration had been seen in the same area in 1900. When pure white the form is ab. *albida*, and a specimen was taken at Camborne in 1961.

Meadow Brown *Maniola jurtina*

No. of tetrads (1995–2000): 444
Status in Cornwall: resident
Regional priority: none
Regional rate of change: increasing, +7%

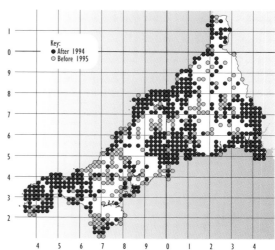

Key:
● After 1994
○ Before 1995

DISTRIBUTION IN CORNWALL

The Meadow Brown is marginally Cornwall's second commonest butterfly, being distributed in slightly less tetrads than the Red Admiral, but in more than the Large and Small Whites, and in every 10km square; it is yet another example where the distribution map shows the density of recorders, and not that of the butterfly.

HABITAT AND ECOLOGY

The butterfly can be met almost anywhere, including urban parks and gardens; indeed, until a year or two ago a small plot of rough grass, behind Penpol Terrace in the centre of Hayle, regularly supported a colony, until the owners decided that it should be kept mown. It has also been seen on Camborne railway station. More normally it inhabits open grassland of almost any type except a mono-culture, providing that it has not been too much improved; grassy heaths, dunes, hedgerows and open rides and glades in woodland also provide habitats.

The nominate subspecies does not occur in Britain, where, in England, its place is taken by ssp. *insularis*, with other subspecies in Scotland and Ireland. Unfortunately, that is only the beginning of a contentious issue which involves Cornish Meadow Browns. For instance, it is claimed that the Meadow Browns of the Isles of Scilly are yet another subspecies (p.125), ssp. *cassiteridum*, although the difference between them and other mainland, south-western specimens is very slight; they are sometimes indistinguishable. Whether they genuinely belong to a different subspecies is questionable. But additionally, much has been made of the variations in the number, size and position of the hindwing spots, and also of the prominent forewing eye-spot of this butterfly, most recently by Ford (1975b), Dowdeswell (1981), Brakefield (1984) and Brakefield and van Noordwijk (1985). Dowdeswell reckoned that the southern English subspecies (*insularis*) extended through Devon almost as far as the Tamar where his east Cornish type, or 'stabilisation', began to appear; the pattern differed again in west Cornwall. The boundary

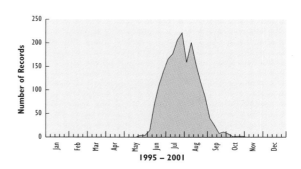

1995 – 2001

between one stabilisation and another could be abrupt, such as between two fields, but could also fluctuate annually, often with intermediate types in between. In Cornwall it would seem that the number of hindwing spots on the female varies between none and three, with none to two predominating, in contrast with a preponderance of none in ssp. *insularis* (p. 125). Several suggestions have been made as to why this variation, if indeed it is significant, should occur, but so far no general agreement has been reached.

The butterfly has a long flight period, but seemingly with only a single brood which, in Cornwall, can run from mid-May until the end of October. This is caused by a lack of synchronisation in the development of the larvae, due partly to the long period of egg-laying and possibly to different types of habitat. For instance, a mating pair was observed at Upton Towans as late as 26 October 1999 which, if the first specimens were seen in early June, would give a flight period extending to nearly five months.

As with other Browns, the adults are often active in dull weather and have even been seen in light rain.

CAUSES OF DECLINE OR INCREASE

Some colonies, as at Hayle, have been lost due to the destruction of the habitat by over-zealous mowing; other agricultural improvements to grassland, including the re-seeding of some meadows with monocultural Rye-grass (*Lolium* spp.) have also destroyed colonies.

CONSERVATION

No specific conservation methods are needed, except to ensure that some areas of natural and semi-natural grassland are maintained.

LARVAL FOODPLANTS

A wide range of grasses is used, although those with finer leaves are preferred, particularly in the earlier stages of larval development: the Fescues (*Festuca* spp.) and Meadow-grasses (*Poa* spp.). Larger larvae will consume Cock's-foot (*Dactylis glomerata*) and False Brome (*Brachypodium sylvaticum*), and possibly other coarser species.

ABERRATIONS

As already indicated there is variation between the subspecies, although not on a regularly definable basis, especially where an interface occurs between them. Moreover, aberrations can also occur within each subspecies. Thus, a butterfly with the characteristics that are typical of one subspecies, when occurring in the geographical area of another, can be regarded as an aberration. Apart from the spotting on the hindwings, variations can also occur in the colour, and a specimen of ab. *pallidus*, in which the ground colour was very pale, was recorded at Bude in 1908. A female, also with very pale patches on the forewings, was seen at Par in 1994, but this may have been caused by a pathological malformation of the scales.

These genuine colour aberrations should not be confused with adult butterflies which have been on the wing for some time, as these tend to bleach with age.

The poor number of aberrations recorded for this very common and variable species in Cornwall is perhaps due to lack of detailed and critical observations.

Ringlet *Aphantopus hyperantus*

No. of tetrads (1995–2000): 139
Status in Cornwall: resident
Regional priority: none
Regional rate of change: increasing, +27%

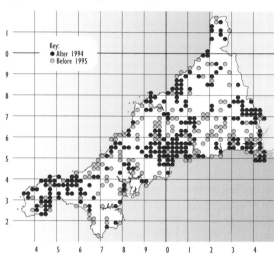

Key:
● After 1994
○ Before 1995

DISTRIBUTION IN CORNWALL

The Ringlet is sometimes thought of as a woodland species, inhabiting the fringes and partly-shaded rides and clearings; but this is certainly not so in Cornwall where there are few woods, and where it can be met with in almost any rural areas. Only two full and five part 10km squares, mainly on the coast, have not produced specimens since 1995. Nevertheless it is scarcer, if not entirely absent from the higher parts of Bodmin Moor and Carnmenellis, and from the Lizard, but occurs in the scrubby areas of the north coast dunes. It forms sizeable colonies, although some can be quite small, numbering no more than a few specimens extending thinly over a distance along bridleways or footpaths.

HABITAT AND ECOLOGY

The Ringlet is one of those curious butterflies which scatters its eggs indiscriminately into the air, either while it is on the wing, or else at rest high on a grass stem. The eggs are non-adhesive and therefore fall directly into the warmer base of the foodplant, where they are concealed from predators; attempts to find them usually fail. The larva, in which stage it passes the winter, continues to feed on mild days, as with some other Browns.

The adult butterfly can be expected almost anywhere, but it is more common in damp, half-shaded, sheltered places, be they hedgerows, combes, dunes or woodland clearings. It is fond of bracken and European Gorse scrub. As with some other dark-coloured butterflies, it can often be found flying on cloudy days, even sometimes in light rain.

The Ringlet is one of the most consistent of butterflies, seldom appearing before the last week of May and usually disappearing by mid August. However, in Cornwall the flight period can be extended back into mid May, while some battered specimens survive until the end of August. There is only one brood.

CAUSES OF DECLINE OR INCREASE

The Ringlet's retreat and its absence from some areas, such as the higher moors, seems to have been amply compensated by

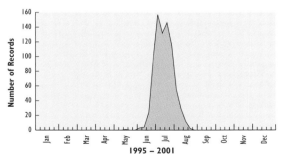

1995 – 2001

its appearance in others. A suspicion must remain that recently it has been under-recorded in places from which it seems to have disappeared.

CONSERVATION

Although the Ringlet appears to be holding its own, if not actually expanding its range in Cornwall, the same factors apply as to the Gatekeeper (p. 111): maintenance and extension of hedges bounding footpaths, bridleways and tracks, throughout the county, in a sympathetic manner.

LARVAL FOODPLANTS

The Ringlet will accept a wide variety of grasses when in captivity, but in the wild it is more specific, apparently using only Cock's-foot (*Dactylis glomerata*) and False Brome (*Brachypodium sylvaticum*), although the latter is missing from the main granite areas of the county, where its place is probably taken by Sheep's-fescue (*Festuca ovina*). Tufted Hair-grass (*Deschampsia cespitosa*) and Creeping Bent (*Agrostis stolonifera*) have also been reported. But apparently the prime requirement for whatever grass is used should be that it grows in lush uncropped tussocks.

ABERRATIONS

The adult butterfly is subject to many aberrations, most of which involve the size and character of the spots of the hindwings. Ab. *arete*, where the spots are reduced to white dots, was recorded at Wheal Rose, Scorrier in 1956. Ab. *crassipuncta*, where the spots are abnormally large, is said to be commoner in the west of England (Penhallurick 1996) although no actual specimens have been recorded. Rarer is ab. *lanceolata*, where the eyes are elongated to a pear-shape, with the point facing toward the outer edge of the wing; one was taken at Mullion in 1899. Aberrations involving the ground colour and the insect size are known, but none have been seen in Cornwall.

Small Heath *Coenonympha pamphilus*

No. of tetrads (1995–2000): 133
Status in Cornwall: resident
Regional priority: none
Regional rate of change: stable; probably slight increase, +5%

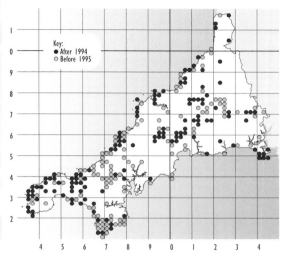

Key:
● After 1994
◎ Before 1995

DISTRIBUTION IN CORNWALL

The Small Heath is widespread throughout much of the county, but with gaps in its distribution along the south coast and in much of the wooded Tamar valley. The coastal slope and cliffs between Marazion and Porthgwarra are now much built upon, with the remainder dominated by bracken and brambles. Many of the gaps on the distribution map though, may be due to under-recording.

HABITAT AND ECOLOGY

The species occupies a variety of habitats, and in Cornwall it can be found on both grassy heaths as well as dunes, so long as the sites are dry and well-drained and where the sward is not too dense. Although it is noted as breeding at a higher altitude than most other butterflies (Asher *et al.* 2001), the colonies seek out sheltered places with a south or south-western aspect.

The breeding pattern is complicated. The first adults may be seen in Cornwall in very late April or May and continue into June; these produce eggs, some of which develop rapidly and give rise to a partial second brood after about four months in August and September and even October. The remainder over-winter as larvae in various stages of development to produce adults after 12 months in the following spring. But the second, rapidly-developing brood of butterflies lay eggs which do not produce adults until the following July, thus almost overlapping the tail of the spring brood (South 1906). Thus it is possible to see the Small Heath at any time from the end of April until mid-October. It is worth noting though, that in parts of west Cornwall, especially in good summers, the numbers of the second brood far exceed those of the first, resulting in a dearth of spring specimens the following year; this would suggest that most of that year's insects had undergone rapid four-month development, leaving only a minority, if any, to go through the full 12-month cycle.

1995 – 2001

CONSERVATION

Agricultural improvements and changes to grazing regimes of grasslands, particularly inland, have no doubt led to the loss of colonies in the past. The re-introduction of more sympathetic regimes by landowners, such as those now being implemented by the National Trust at Kenidjack, will help to ensure that suitable habitats continue to exist.

LARVAL FOODPLANTS
Most fine-bladed grasses will serve, especially Fescues (*Festuca* spp.), Meadow-grasses (*Poa* spp.) and Bents (*Agrostis* spp.), all of which are well represented in the county by one species or another.

ABERRATIONS
Aberration in the Small Heath is not uncommon, though few have been recorded in Cornwall. An example of ab. *partimtransformis*, where white patches occur on the wings, symmetrically in this example, was taken at Rough Tor near Camelford in 1937.

Monarch *Danaus plexippus*

No. of tetrads (1995–2000): 57
Status in Cornwall: involuntary immigrant, vagrant
Regional priority: none
Regional rate of change: not assessed

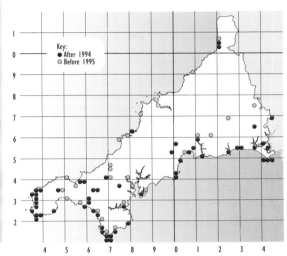

Key:
● After 1994
○ Before 1995

DISTRIBUTION IN CORNWALL

The Monarch is a remarkable immigrant which travels nearly 6,000km across the Atlantic to reach these shores from its homelands in north America, although some of the specimens seen in this country may originate in the Canary Islands, Madeira or southern Spain, where it is now resident.

It would seem that most Monarchs which enter Britain come as the result of weather conditions on the eastern seaboard of the Americas, and are often connected with autumn hurricanes; the latter usually arrive in this country, after crossing the Atlantic as deep depressions with westerly gales, and bring the butterflies with them. Monarchs have been observed occasionally at sea off the Cornish coast, most notably by the cruise liner Canberra 130km west of the Isles of Scilly and in the Atlantic by the passengers and crews of RMS Queen Mary and RMS Queen Elizabeth; they have also been seen by passengers on MV Scillonian on its crossing to the Scillies.

With this background, it is not surprising that the greatest number of specimens recorded in Britain is seen in Cornwall and the Isles of Scilly, and the distribution is becoming fairly regular and to some extent predictable, especially in years of large influxes. The butterfly occurs most frequently in the tetrads surrounding the Scillies and the Land's End peninsula, and additionally in those of the south coast; only few occur, or are detected, in the inland tetrads. Thus virtually all west Cornwall has multiple records, whereas relatively few butterflies are seen in east Cornwall away from the south coast. Other places, where numbers can

be expected, are on the promontory headlands projecting into the English Channel, such as Gwennap Head, Cudden Point, the Lizard, Dodman Point, Gribben Head and Rame Head.

HABITAT AND ECOLOGY

The butterfly, once it has made a landfall, does not seem to stray far inland. It is notably attracted to garden and coastal Buddleja (*Buddleja davidii*) and Sedum (*Sedum spectabile*); it will take up a territory for several days, while making occasional exploratory flights in the local neighbourhood. The butterflies have been observed to roost in the same tree on several

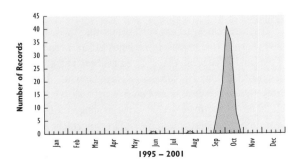

1995 – 2001

successive nights. Some may move on to new localities, with a significant change of wind, both towards eastern, or northern counties or even southward to north-west Europe. Their foodplant is absent from Britain, so that their main habitat is sheltered nectaring sites with adjacent trees mainly on or near the coast.

In its homelands of north America, the Monarch breeds intermittently on its long migratory flights north from Mexico in the spring and its subsequent return in the autumn; most of the specimens seen in Britain are migrants from the latter movement. Consequently it is most likely to be reported in Cornwall from August to November, with a peak of appearances in September and October; very occasionally specimens have been recorded as early as March, but they may have been captive-bred escapes or releases, or vagrants from the northwards spring migrations in America.

CAUSES OF DECLINE OR INCREASE

Much depends on the weather on the other side of the north Atlantic for the Monarch's appearance in Cornwall, although sunny and calm conditions in the county probably lead to more sightings, especially in the years of large migrations. Numbers are notoriously difficult to estimate owing to the butterflies' mobility; many records may be duplicates of the same individual seen at several different points. But a real increase has occurred since 1980.

CONSERVATION

Little can be done to help this migrant in Britain, since the larval foodplant is absent; but ensuring that gardeners near the south coast maintain an ample supply of autumnal nectar sources would be beneficial. Suggestions have been made for the planting of Milkweed spp. (*Asclepias* spp.) in gardens, where they would probably survive in the comparatively frost-free environment of the south coast.

LARVAL FOODPLANTS

Larvae feed on Milkweeds (*Asclepias* spp.) and there does not appear to be an alternative which would be available to them in this country. Females originating from a nearby butterfly centre were seen to deposit eggs on three species of Milkweeds at the Royal Botanical Gardens, Kew in 1982; adults emerged from some of these eggs in about a month.

ABERRATIONS

Any aberrations which may occur are unknown from the relatively few specimens reaching Cornwall.

OCCURRENCES IN CORNWALL

The bare details of sightings in Cornwall down to 1995 are contained in Penhallurick (1996) and F.H.N. Smith (1997); but some individual experiences may help to fill out these accounts of the Monarch's arrivals in 1995 and later years.

In late September of 1995 a sequence of three hurricanes off the eastern coast of north America resulted in strong westerly airflows extending to north-west Europe. Massive numbers of Monarchs were reported assembling in New Jersey on 28 September, which, in conjunction with the wind, resulted in the first individuals being sighted in Cornwall on 3 October, continuing over the next four days, and followed by a peak of at least twenty on 8 October. On that day three were seen at Hannafore Point, Looe, with another three at Kynance Cove. Further daily sightings continued until 17 October, when the last specimen to arrive in Cornwall was recorded at Gover Valley, St Austell, making a total of 52 individuals recorded in Cornwall during the year.

The next three years saw very few butterflies arrive but in 1999 another sequence of hurricanes crossed the United States at just the right time, and resulted in an influx of Monarchs in the county. The first were seen in the Isles of Scilly and the western tip of the Land's End peninsula on 22 September and the last at Rame Head on 22 October. A total count of 129 butterflies were seen in a period of thirty-one successive days in Cornwall, the largest and longest invasion so far recorded in Britain (Tunmore 2000). Between these two dates several notable sightings occurred. Two butterflies took up residence in a garden at Portmellon between 23–29 September; these were observed roosting in a nearby sycamore tree, then descending each morning to nectar on sedums, where one was photographed (*Butterfly Conservation News* 2000). Elsewhere, six Monarchs were seen flying south at Loe Pool on 5 October while another four were noted on buddleja at Coverack between 4–6 October. After 12 October sightings became increasingly restricted to the Isles of Scilly.

This invasion was one of the largest and longest recorded in the British history of the butterfly, with three main peaks appearing on 24–25 September, 3–6 October and 11–12 October, all dates which coincided with favourable weather in the county; over 300 arrivals were recorded in Britain.

There were few records in 2000, although 2001 again saw an increase, but nowhere on the scale of 1999. The first arrivals were in August, which was unusually early, but surprisingly none were then seen in Cornwall, and it was not until 1 October that the first butterflies appeared. Between 1 October and 3 November, 35 were provisionally recorded in the county (Insect Line 2001), with the last at Ruan Minor. The latest arrival so far was one seen at Angarrack on 12 November 2002.

CHAPTER 5

EXOTICA

Some unexpected butterflies in Cornwall and very unusual migrants

The butterfly species in the foregoing accounts are all included in good faith as genuine natural occurrences in the county, and, with some luck, they might all be seen again. There remains a handful of butterflies which have appeared in the county, but which were never resident, or are not resident now for a variety of reasons; some are never likely to be seen again. Some extremely rare and unusual migrants are included. All are included in this chapter to complete the record (Penhallurick 1996; Smith, F.H.N. 1997).

In the middle of May 1996, a female **Chequered Skipper** (*Carterocephalus palaemon*) was seen on Gwithian Green. It was observed both in flight and at rest for the best part of half-an-hour. Several clumps of False Brome grass (*Brachypodium sylvaticum*) were then seen in the vicinity, in which it displayed an interest; unfortunately the clumps shortly after succumbed to over-enthusiastic clearance of Japanese Knotweed (*Fallopia japonica*). But the butterfly must have been captive-bred and subsequently released or escaped; later searches all failed to locate others then, or in following years.

In September 2001, a lethargic continental **Swallowtail** (*Papilio machaon gorganus*) was recovered from Chymorvah Vean, near Marazion, which eventually revived and was allowed to fly away. A few days before, at the end of August, another specimen had been reported at Marazion Marsh. Despite the fact that two larvae of *P. machaon gorganus* were located in a Kentish garden in 2000 (Maddocks 2002), which produced adults in 2001, the Marazion species may have been produced by a local breeder, who was operating in the area. Nevertheless, there is a slim chance that they could have been genuine migrants.

There are also records of an **Apollo** (*Parnassius apollo*) at Mylor about 1826, and of the **Scarce Swallowtail** (*Iphiclides podalarius*) from Landulph Marsh in 1971 and near Ludgvan in 1974.

A specimen of the **Cleopatra** (*Gonepteryx cleopatra*) was captured at Feock in September 1957. Although occasionally occurring in Britain, it is not a naturally migratory species and is usually assumed to have received an 'assisted' passage. Feock lies close to the river Fal, where, in recent decades, it has been the custom to lay-up surplus merchant ships as far up-river as the King Harry ferry.

There have been very occasional surprising sightings of the **Chalkhill Blue** (*Polyommatus (Lysandra) coridon*) in Cornwall, particularly so since the larval foodplant, Horseshoe Vetch (*Hippocrepis comosa*) does not grow in the county. Most of the occurrences were in the nineteenth or early twentieth century. Since then a worn specimen was seen at Kennack Sands, just east of Lizard Point in 1947; it was the only one in the last century, and was probably a genuine vagrant from Devon or Dorset, since the butterfly used to breed in the former county.

The **Duke of Burgundy** (*Hamearis lucina*) was recorded in the early part of the last century in the east of the county, but the last was seen in 1956 at Bodinnick, east of Fowey.

The **American Painted Lady** (*Cynthia virginiensis*) has appeared in Cornwall a few times, either as a genuine trans-Atlantic visitor, or else from the Canary Islands or Portugal, where it is said to be resident (Bustillo and Fernandez-Rubio 1974). Two probables were recorded near St Austell in 1995 and 2000 (Lane 2000b), and another at St Agnes in the Scillies in 1998.

The **Purple Emperor** (*Apatura iris*) is of uncertain status in Cornwall, with most sightings being of captive-bred escapes or releases, such as three seen near Land's End in 1988. More recently, in 1998, another was observed near Feock and watched for 30 minutes on the bonnet of a car; also seen were two others described as either female Purple Emperors or White Admirals.

Several **Mediterranean Fritillaries** (*Argynnis pandora*) were seen near Tintagel in 1911, one of which was captured. It is an extremely rare migrant, which does not even feature in the Millennium Atlas (Asher *et al*. 2001).

On 12 August 2002, the first **Geranium Bronze** (*Cacyreus marshalli*) to be recorded in Cornwall was seen in a garden at Gwithian. Apparently the next-door neighbours were in the habit of taking a couple of pots of Pelargoniums to southern Spain, to ornament their holiday home, and then returning with them. Undoubtedly an egg, larva or pupa had hitched a passage as well.

CHAPTER 6

BUTTERFLIES OF
THE ISLES OF SCILLY

It is well known that islands generally have lower biodiversity than mainland areas of a similar size. In mainland areas, species can easily move into new districts, whereas on islands colonisation of new areas is more difficult especially for the least mobile animals. Species diversity on an island generally depends on its area and distance from the mainland. The number of species living on an island is also a balance between immigration and extinction. Islands can trap new species which can successfully colonise the available habitat, but, because many of these populations are small, they can become extinct as quickly as they began. Once a species becomes extinct, re-establishment can be difficult because there are no adjacent reservoir colonies. However, if habitats and other factors remain constant, an equilibrium can be reached, a balance between rates of extinction and immigration. The chance of new species arriving becomes less as the total number present rises, as most of the immigrants will be from those already there. In fact, many of the plants and animals on Scilly probably arrived either overland before the islands were formed or were introduced deliberately or accidentally by people (Spalding and Sargeant 2000).

The number of butterfly species on Scilly is considerably less than found in Cornwall. The list of moths and butterflies published by the Isles of Scilly Museum Association (Agassiz 1981) includes 19 species of butterfly. This number has now been increased to 26, perhaps partly as a result of increased levels of recording but also because new species regularly fly across the sea from abroad. Indeed, the Isles of Scilly are excellent places from which to observe migrant moths and butterflies and many of the records of migrant lepidoptera are made by so-called 'twitchers' looking for migrant birds.

A brief review of the history of the islands is instructive when considering the number and position of butterflies here. Around 18,000 years ago, during the coldest part of the Ice Age when the sea level was approximately 130m lower than today, the islands were part of the British mainland. They, together with Cornwall and southern England, would have been free of ice, but the soil would have been frozen and have supported only tundra. As the ice thawed at the beginning of the post-glacial period, sea levels here rose to about 35–40 metres below present levels and the land bridge between Scilly and Cornwall was drowned. At this time, around 10,000 BC, Scilly may have consisted of one large island (Thomas, A.C. 1985). As the ice sheets continued to melt, the rising sea submerged the low-lying land and led to the creation, by 3000 BC, of a number of separate islands, with one large island encompassing St Mary's, Bryher, Tresco and St Martin's; St Agnes, Annet and Western Rocks constituted three smaller islands. It may not have been until the fifth or sixth centuries AD that today's islands began to appear.

It is probable that some at least of the butterflies found here colonised the islands across the land-bridge that formed as the ice melted. Those species that have developed unique subspecies or races such as Meadow Brown and Common Blue have probably been on Scilly for many hundreds of years. Unique subspecies are found in other insect groups also, e.g. Scilly Bee (*Bombus muscorum scyllonius*). Colonisation is more difficult now that the land-bridge has disappeared, although some butterflies appear to be recent arrivals. One example is the Holly Blue, a well-known wanderer, but not recorded on Scilly until 1977 at St Mary's and 1978 at Tresco. There has been a long tradition of deliberately introducing wildlife species to the island (e.g. the elder tree and the budgerigar) and there have been many accidental imports (e.g. the Prickly Stick-insect and the New Zealand Flatworm). It is not known however if any butterflies have been introduced in this manner.

Even for such a well-studied group as the butterflies, it can be difficult to decide whether individual species are wanderers, transitory or permanent residents of the islands. For example, the Small Heath, which is perhaps the commonest and most widespread butterfly in Britain, has only been seen rarely on Scilly and is unlikely to be resident (Penhallurick 1996). Other species which are likely to be vagrant here are the Orange-tip and Green-veined White (Table 4). In fact, between 12 and 13 species are probably resident. Of course, any species arriving on Scilly would only be able to become resident if there was suitable habitat and if they could survive the warm winters, cool summers and exposure to the influence of the prevailing westerly winds. The islands contain fewer habitats than mainland Britain, the main habitats being cultivated fields, pasture, heathland and coastal dunes. Woodland is absent on Scilly apart from a conifer plantation on Tresco, so that woodland butterflies are absent; there are no fritillaries here.

Many of the butterflies are mobile species found on most of the islands. Dennis and Shreeve (1996) list butterflies found on each island but there appear to be no records for many of the smaller islands such as Annet and Rosevear. Amongst the most widespread species are Small White, Red Admiral and Painted Lady, which move around Scilly with ease and may be regularly seen from the passenger ferries moving between the islands. Small and Large Whites are found everywhere, and these populations are probably reinforced by summer influxes. The Small Copper is one of the commonest butterflies late in the year; the blue-spotted ab. *caeruleopunctata* occurs in small numbers. The Comma is another wanderer, living in open populations. It too may be a recent arrival here, following its expansion over the last 80 years in southern Britain.

Other butterflies are more sedentary, such as the Green-veined White and Common Blue, and are therefore more likely to be prone to local extinctions. Work on populations of the Common Blue by Ford and Dowdeswell in 1938 (Dowdeswell 1981) has led to suggestions that the 300m sea gap between Tean and St Martin's was an effective barrier to movement. They also suggested that Common Blues here were more variable in the spotting on the underside of the wings, especially the males; this is perhaps likely to be more a factor of the butterfly being at the edge of its range than one of genetic isolation. However, Ford (1975) suggested that a remarkable race existed on Tean where females caught in the summer had a scattering of pale silvery-blue scales; however there is no recent evidence of this form and most Common Blues appear identical to the mainland forms. It is difficult to explain the

Table 4. A brief list of butterflies recorded on Scilly.

Name	Resident/ migrant	Summary of records
American Painted Lady	M	St Agnes, 1998
Bath White	M	St Mary's, in 1977
Brimstone	M	recorded in 1911, 1977, 1984
Camberwell Beauty	M	St Mary's in 1983
Clouded Yellow	M	widely recorded migrant
Comma	R?	first recorded in 1971, then 1981 and 1982
Common Blue	R	regularly recorded
Green-veined White	R?	sporadically recorded, e.g. on Gugh, St Mary's
Holly Blue	R	first recorded in 1977
Large Tortoiseshell	M	Tresco in 1934
Large White	R/M	widely recorded
Long-tailed Blue	M	St Mary's, 1996
Meadow Brown	R	widely recorded
Monarch	M	occasional, but more commonly recorded recently 1995–1999
Orange-tip	M?	recorded on St Mary's in 1986
Painted Lady	M	regularly recorded
Pale Clouded Yellow	M	rare migrant
Peacock	R	widely recorded
Red Admiral	M	regularly recorded
Ringlet	R	St Martin's from the mid-1990s
Small Copper	R	widely recorded
Small Heath	M?	rare
Small Tortoiseshell	R	widely recorded
Small White	R/M	widely recorded
Speckled Wood	R	widely recorded
Wall	R	occasional

presence on Scilly of these sedentary species. Some of the less mobile British species, such as the Hairstreaks and the Skippers, have never been recorded here, although several of them could probably survive once they reached the islands. For example, the Green Hairstreak lives in Cornwall on maritime Gorse scrub which is abundant on Scilly, and this lovely butterfly would probably thrive here. Dennis and Shreeve (1996) suggest that most if not all British butterfly species have the capacity to migrate to nearby offshore islands, even if only occasionally when migrations coincide with extreme weather events. The existence of populations of Silver-studded Blue and Marsh Fritillary in west Penwith suggest that these species may yet turn up on Scilly.

The islands are excellent places to see migrant butterflies such as Painted Lady, which is often abundant as in 1996, and the Clouded Yellow; however, records of Berger's Clouded Yellow must remain in doubt without voucher specimens. The American Painted Lady was recorded on St Agnes in September 1998. The Large Tortoiseshell recorded floating on the sea off Tresco in 1934 after a south-easterly gale was certainly a migrant, as was the Camberwell Beauty recorded on St Mary's in 1983. Sightings of Monarchs used to be rare, but they have been seen every year since 1995. Red Admirals are also migrants, flying northwards from continental Europe in spring and southwards again from mid-August onwards. Early sightings (e.g. on 14 January on St Agnes) are likely to be of hibernating individuals that have successfully over-wintered, but there is no proof that they can survive here (Hicks and Hale 1998); perhaps the winter climate is generally too mild and wet.

MEADOW BROWN

The Meadow Brown on Scilly is generally brighter than the mainland race and has been given subspecific status (*Maniola jurtina cassiteridum*); it is similar to the Irish subspecies. It is a common butterfly on Scilly and can be abundant where it occurs. For example, Dowdeswell and Ford (Dowdeswell 1981) estimated that maximum numbers of Meadow Browns flying on Tean in 1938 were around 8,650, flying in three isolated colonies. Meadow Browns have been recorded on St Agnes, Bryher, St Helen's, Tresco, St Martin's, Tean, Great Arthur, White Island, St Mary's, Gugh, Samson, Menawethan, Great Innisvouls and Great Ganilly. There is a large variation between individuals in the number and position of small spots on the underside hindwing (varying from none to five), which is controlled by genes. Spot variation appears to be greater on the large islands which have a wider range of environments than on the smaller isolated islands where natural selection has produced a gene complex adapted to specific conditions. For example, females on St Martin's, Tresco and St Mary's generally have either none, one or two spots on the hindwing, whereas most females have two hindwing spots on St Helen's and no spots on White Island. Hindwing spot patterns vary on Tean between none and two spots. The genetic make-up which produces the spot variation also affects seasonal emergence times and larval growth rates so that individuals with fewer spots tend to be associated with slow-growing caterpillars and emergence late in the season. There is also a link between the number of hindwing spots and the size of the forewing eyespot, which can be used to scare predators away or to divert attacks onto the spot rather than the body.

SPECKLED WOOD

The Speckled Wood was first recorded on Scilly at Tresco in 1903 and was included in a list made in 1925 for Tresco. There appear to be no other records until 1967 (Penhallurick 1996), when it was recorded on St Agnes. It is now common on the larger islands. It is interesting to note that the Speckled Wood underwent a dramatic reduction in range in Britain in the late nineteenth and early twentieth centuries, before increasing from the 1920s onwards. This change in its range may have been replicated on Scilly, but there are too few records for this to be substantiated. However, it certainly seems to be commoner on Scilly than formerly, and has now been recorded from Bryher, Gugh, St Agnes, St Martin's, St Mary's, Tean and Tresco.

The Speckled Wood has been allotted separate subspecific status as *Pararge aegeria insula*, described from a colony found on St Mary's in 1969 and 1970 as having orange rather than yellow markings. They are more like the southern European subspecies *aegeria* than the mainland British subspecies *tircis*. However, these differences can appear slight in the field, especially on old worn specimens where the colour has faded. The existence in collections of bright specimens may be at least partly due to the fact that collectors tend to favour the most extreme forms and discard the yellower specimens. Although a woodland edge species in much of Britain, in the maritime climate of Scilly and Cornwall, Speckled Woods are generally associated with any area where shade occurs, e.g. hedgerows and isolated trees, and its bright colour may be an adaptation to this more open habitat. On St Agnes, for example, it is most common under trees but can be found all over the island (Hicks and Hale 1998).

CHAPTER 7

WHERE BEST TO SEE BUTTERFLIES IN CORNWALL

Many species of butterflies can still be seen in Cornwall; over 40 are still commonly resident, while it is probably the best county in Britain to see both common and unusual migrants.

During the spring, over-wintering species such as **Peacock**, **Small Tortoiseshell**, **Comma**, **Brimstone** and occasional **Red Admiral**, can be observed quite regularly as early as March, or even February, together with the occasional newly-emerged **Speckled Wood** and **Holly Blue**, at any number of places in the county.

In the first weeks of May, Cornwall's countryside explodes with an array of butterfly specialities. Although the county has lost 80% of its **Pearl-bordered Fritillary** colonies during the last 25 years, this nationally threatened species can still be seen from early May on the undercliff coastal footpath between Millendreath and Seaton, below the Murrayton Monkey Sanctuary; the stretch of path east of the coastal woodland is a favourite habitat. This same stretch later in the summer is also an excellent place for migrants, such as **Clouded Yellows**, **Painted Ladies** and **Monarchs**.

Bunny's Hill, near Cardinham, holds one of Cornwall's largest colonies of **Pearl-bordered Fritillaries**, which was only discovered in 1998. The butterfly can be seen here at close range within 18m of the road, so the site is most suitable for the elderly or infirm. This area of common land also supports **Dingy Skippers** and, later in the year, **Dark Green** and **Silver-washed Fritillaries**. Photography is comparatively easy.

Late May and June is the best time to visit the Cornwall Wildlife Trust's reserve at Breney Common, where probably the largest colony of **Marsh Fritillaries** is to be found in the county. **Small Pearl-bordered Fritillaries** also thrive here at about the same time, while slightly later the heathland **Silver-studded Blue**, the **Small Skipper**, **Ringlets** and **Dark Green Fritillary** can be seen, as well as a host of more common species.

The Duchy of Cornwall's reserve at Greenscombe Wood, Luckett is home to one of only two colonies of **Heath Fritillaries** in Cornwall, where it can be seen both in coppiced woodland and in grassy meadows; it is a nationally rare and high priority species. It emerges slightly earlier here than in Somerset or Kent and can usually be seen from mid-May. Later in the year, large numbers of **Marbled Whites** appear; here they are almost at the extreme westerly limit of their range in Britain.

A place to see **Grizzled Skippers** is on the recently-discovered site along a disused railway track on the western edge of Goss Moor near Indian Queens. It is not far from Breney Common and both could be visited in one day.

One of the largest colonies of **Green Hairstreaks** is at Penlee Point, part of which is again a Cornwall Wildlife Trust reserve. Later in the year, **Marbled Whites** can be seen in good numbers, together with any migrants that might appear on this coastal site.

In west Cornwall there are perhaps half-a-dozen coastal sites which are worth visiting both in the spring and early summer and again in the later summer and autumn.

The stretch of coast between Porthleven and Perranuthnoe is good for **Small Pearl-bordered Fritillary** and **Walls** in May and June, while **Dark Green Fritillary**, **Brown**

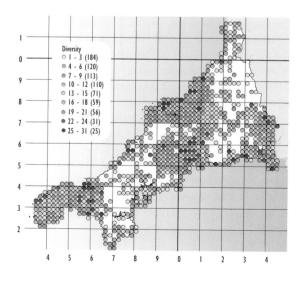

Diversity
○ 1 - 3 (184)
○ 4 - 6 (120)
● 7 - 9 (113)
○ 10 - 12 (110)
● 13 - 15 (71)
● 16 - 18 (59)
● 19 - 21 (56)
● 22 - 24 (31)
● 25 - 31 (25)

Total number of butterfly species recorded in Cornwall, per tetrad (1995–2000).

Argus and **Grayling** can be observed later in the year. Easy access can be gained at Rinsey Cove and Cudden Point; just east of the latter is one of the largest coastal heathland populations of **Silver-studded Blue** in Cornwall; also to be seen at both Rinsey and Cudden Point is the unusual second brood of the **Small Pearl-bordered Fritillary**, mainly in August.

Another good place, especially for incoming migrants, is near the south-west corner of England, Gwennap Head, a kilometre of so west of Porthgwarra, near which is one of the few **Marsh Fritillary** colonies in west Cornwall. **Small Pearl-bordered Fritillaries** can be seen early in the summer, but better times to visit are July, August and September when

A butterfly haven at Pontsmill, Lanlivery.

Graylings and **Dark Green Fritillaries** abound. It is also the first landfall site for many migrants and **Painted Ladies**, **Clouded Yellows**, **Pale Clouded Yellows**, **Bath Whites** (the last in Cornwall was seen here in August 1996) and **Monarchs** are all possible. A walk from Gwennap Head northwards to Carn Guthensbrâs will produce another colony of **Silver-studded Blues** and a multitude of **Graylings.**

North of Cape Cornwall is an area which was once heavily industrialised with mine workings. The easiest point of access is probably at Botallack, which can be reached by taking the lane and track northwards from the centre of the village. Here begins a series of **Silver-studded Blue** colonies, which extend as far as Pendeen Watch. The largest is behind Wheal Cock, where may also be seen, in season, large numbers of **Graylings**, **Dark Green Fritillaries**, **Brown Argus**, **Small Heaths** and other more common species, as well as migrants.

Cornwall boasts some of Britain's highest sand dune systems on its north coast. One is located between Perranporth and Holywell Bay and includes Penhale and Gear Sands; some of the area has restricted access owing to the military activities of Penhale Training Camps. Most dune systems are calcareous, consisting mainly of crushed seashells, with the result that they support a flora nowhere else seen in the county. A visit here in May will be rewarded by many **Brown Argus** and possibly also by the **Grizzled Skipper**, in one of only two of its main sites in Cornwall. It is only found in small numbers scattered across the dunes. A high proportion of the adults here are ab. *taras*. **Dingy Skippers** also appear. But the main claim to fame for these dunes is the huge populations of **Silver-studded Blues** which breed here. Other butterflies to be seen are **Dark Green Fritillaries**, and numerous **Large** and **Small Skippers**, **Common Blues**, **Walls**, **Graylings**, **Small Heaths** and often the commoner migrants.

The second main dune system lies to the east of the river Hayle and includes Phillack, Mexico, Upton and Gwithian Towans. Here the picture is much the same as at Penhale and Gear Sands, but for the absence of the **Grizzled Skipper**, and with the addition of the **Small Pearl-bordered Fritillary**; its second brood here is particularly noticeable, and often out-numbers the first. Again there are big colonies of the **Silver-studded Blue**, which were first shown at Upton Towans to have a second brood at the end of August. Gwithian Towans also produced one of the first records of an **Essex Skipper** in west Cornwall.

On the Lizard peninsula, the most productive site to visit in August is Kynance Cove, close to the most southerly point of mainland Britain. Boasting a particularly mild climate, it often attracts incoming migrants, which make their first landfall in the neighbourhood. **Monarchs** appear almost every year between August and October, together with **Clouded Yellows**, **Red Admirals** and **Painted Ladies**; the **Long-tailed Blue** was recorded near here in 2001. The last **High Brown Fritillary** to be seen in west Cornwall also appeared here.

In the far north of Cornwall, near the Devon border, lies one of the best nature reserves for butterflies, Welcombe and Marsland, managed by the Devon Wildlife Trust. The area of extensive woodland, with sheltered glades and valley bottoms is an excellent place to see **Pearl-** and **Small Pearl-bordered Fritillaries**, **Silver-washed Fritillary** and possibly even the scarce **High Brown Fritillary**.

To conclude, Cornwall possesses a wide variety of suitable habitats for many butterflies and there is always the chance of the visitor discovering a new colony of one of the county's rare species. Please send your records to the Branch Recorder.

DIRECTIONS FOR ACCESS TO SITES MENTIONED ABOVE

Botallack (SW 363337)
Take the B 3306 along the coast north from St Just or south from St Ives; take the road into the village and then the turning for Manor Farm. Pass the farm and go on to the National Trust centre, beyond which the disused mine works begin. Park here. Walk north to Crown Rocks and Wheal Cock beyond, and then north again to Pendeen Watch.

Breney Common (SX 054610)
From A30/391 (Innis Downs) roundabout south of Bodmin, turn north to Lanivet; then take the first right and go under the A30 bridge; take first left shortly after the bridge to Reperry Cross; turn right and take the left fork to Trebell Green. From there go on to Gustla, where the entrance track to the reserve is on the left after the Methodist Church. Contact tel: (01872) 273939.

Bunny's Hill, near Cardinham (SX 117675)
From A30 take the A38 road at Bodmin to Liskeard; almost immediately turn left past Glyn Valley crematorium; go through Fletchers Bridge heading north to a fork in the road; park here and proceed on foot.

Cudden Point (SW 552278)
Take south coast road, A394 from Penzance to Helston. Turn off to Prussia Cove at Rosudgeon (opposite Falmouth Packet public house). Park at Prussia Cove car park and proceed on foot to coastal footpath at Prussia Cove. Walk west along path to Cudden Point.

Greenscombe Wood, Luckett (SX 391723)
Take the A390 west from Gunnislake. After 4.5km (3 miles) turn right towards Kelly Bray. At Monkscross turn right to Luckett. Access to the reserve is by the first lane on the right in Luckett. Park in the village car park and walk along track into the wood.

Gwithian and Upton Towans (SW 5739-5741)
Enter Hayle on A30 from the east; on roundabout (Loggans Moor) leave A30 to B3301; immediately turn right at next mini-roundabout towards Gwithian; proceed for 1km (3/4 mile) to a lay-by on the left of the road, from where access may be gained to Upton Towans. For Gwithian Towans proceed further along B3301 for another 1.5km (1 mile) to another lay-by and a car park entrance to the beach.

Kynance Cove (SW 689131)
From A394 turn onto A3083 just south of Helston; skirt Culdrose Fleet Air Arm base and continue on towards the Lizard. An unmetalled track to the right about 1km (3/4 mile) before the village goes to Kynance Cove.

Inland Silver-studded Blue site at Breney Common (left) and Marsh Fritillary site at Goss Moor (right).

Millendreath to Seaton Coastal Path (SX 269541)

Park car at Millendreath Beach car park, reached by unclassified road from B3253, and proceed eastwards along coastal footpath for about 1.5km (1 mile) to wooded valley below the Monkey Sanctuary.

Old Railway, near Indian Queens (SW 937591)

Leave new A30 at Indian Queens roundabout and head back towards Bodmin on old A30, park near the railway bridge at SW 931599. Walk through gateway on south side of the road onto dismantled railway; take right-hand fork.

Penhale and Gear Sands (SW 7655-7659)

Take A392 south from Newquay and join A3075. After 5km (3 miles) turn right to Cubert. Another 5km (3 miles) to a National Trust car park at Holywell Bay Beach at SW 767587, then follow coastal footpath south, avoiding MOD land. Permission to enter the restricted area may be obtained by telephoning (01637) 830343.

Penlee Point (SX 436491)

From Millbrook head for Cawsand and Rame. In Rame turn left just before the church and follow road for 1km (3/4 mile) to the car park.

Porthgwarra (SW 371218)

On A30 from Penzance to Land's End fork left for St Buryan at Catchall. Go through St Buryan to Treen and continue on road going west to Polgigga where there is a sharp right-hand bend; take left turning on the bend to Porthgwarra. Park in the car park there and walk up lane to Coastwatch Station, then follow coast path north to Carn Guthensbrâs; alternatively follow coast path round Gwennap Head from the village, or go eastwards towards St Levan.

Rinsey (SW 594273)

Take main south coast road A394 from Helston to Penzance. Turn left in Ashton and continue to Rinsey; go through hamlet onto rough, unmetalled road to National Trust car park above the Cove. Walk down to the engine house and then continue on the coast path to Trewavas Head and beyond. Alternatively take the coast path going west from the car park to Lesceave.

Welcombe and Marsland Nature Reserve (SS 215175)

Take A39 (Clovelly–Newquay). Turn off westwards at Welcombe Cross to Welcombe. Access by prior arrangement with the Warden, tel: (01288) 331266.

SELECT BIBLIOGRAPHY

Agassiz, D. 1981. *A Revised List of the Lepidoptera of the Isles of Scilly.* Isles of Scilly Museum Association, St. Mary's.

Archer-Locke, A. 1989. 'Butterflies in Winter'. *Entomologist's Record and Journ. of Variation* 101, 117–8.

Asher, J., Warren, M., Fox, R., Harding, P., Jeffcoate, G. and Jeffcoate, S. 2001. *The Millennium Atlas of Butterflies in Britain and Ireland.* Oxford University Press, Oxford.

Barnett, L.K. and Warren, M.S. 1995. *Species Action Plan: High Brown Fritillary Argynnis adippe.* Butterfly Conservation, Wareham.

Barton, R.M. 1964. *An Introduction to the Geology of Cornwall.* Bradford Barton Ltd., Truro.

Berger, L.A. 1948. 'A Colias new to Britain (Lep. Pieridae)'. *Entomologist* 81, 129–131.

Bourn, N.A.D., Warren, M.S. and Kirkland, P. 1996. *Action for Butterflies.* Butterfly Conservation, Wareham.

Bourn, N.A.D. and Warren, M.S. 1998. *Species Action Plan: Brown Hairstreak Thecla betulae.* Butterfly Conservation, Wareham.

Bracken, C.W. 1936. 'Westward Drift of the Comma Butterfly'. *Trans. Devonshire Ass.* 68, 135–7.

Brakefield, P.M. 1984. 'The ecological genetics of quantitative characters of *Maniola jurtina* and other butterflies', in (eds) Vane-Wright, R.I. and Ackery, P.R., *The Biology of Butterflies,* 167–9. London.

Brakefield, P.M. and van Noordwijk, A.J. 1985. 'The genetics of spot pattern characters in the Meadow Brown *Maniola jurtina* (Lepidoptera, Satyrinae)'. *Heredity* 54, 275–84.

Bustillo, M.R.G. and Fernandez-Rubio, F. 1974. *Mariposas de la Peninsula Iberica. Ropaloceros II.* Instituto Nacional Para la Conservacion de la Naturaleza. Ministera de Agricultura, Madrid.

Butterfly Conservation 2000. 'Rare Visitor'. *Butterfly Conservation News* 73, 8.

Butterfly Observer, The. Triannual Newsletter of Cornwall Butterfly Conservation.

Chalmers-Hunt, J.M. and Owen, D.F. 1953. *Nymphalis polychloros* L. (Lep. Nymphalidae) in Kent'. *Entomologist's Gazette* 4, 3–11.

Clark, J. 1906. 'Lepidoptera' in (ed.) Page, W. *Victoria County History of Cornwall, Vol. I,* 203–27. Constable, London.

Clark, S. and Grove, S. 1992. *High Brown Fritillary: Hartland Peninsula and West Exmoor Region 1992.* Unpublished Contract Report for Butterfly Conservation.

Cornwall Biodiversity Initiative 1998. *Cornwall's Biodiversity, Vol. 2 : Action Plans.* Cornwall Wildlife Trust, Truro.

Davy, F.H. 1909. *Flora of Cornwall.* Chegwidden, Penryn.

Dennis, R.L.H. and Shreeve, T.G. 1996. *Butterflies on British and Irish offshore islands : Ecology and Biogeography.* Gem Publishing Co., Wallingford.

Dowdeswell, W.H. 1981. *The Life of the Meadow Brown.* Heinemann Educational Books, London.

Emmet, A.M. and Heath, J. 1990. *The Moths and Butterflies of Grest Britain and Ireland, 7, part 1, the Butterflies.* Harley Books, Colchester.

Ford, E.B. 1975a. (Revised edn.). *Butterflies.* Collins, London.

Ford, E.B. 1975b. *Ecological Genetics (4 edn.).* Chapman and Hall, London.

French, C., Murphy, R. and Atkinson, M. 1999. *Flora of Cornwall.* Wheal Seton Press, Camborne.

Frohawk, F.W. 1924. *The Natural History of British Butterflies,* 2 vols. Hutchinson and Co., London.

Frohawk, F.W. 1934. *The Complete Book of British Butterflies.* Ward, Lock and Co. Ltd., London.

Frohawk, F.W. 1938. *Varieties of British Butterflies.* Ward, Lock and Co. Ltd., London.

Frost, M.P. and Madge, S.C. 1991. *Butterflies in South-East Cornwall.* The Caradon Field and Natural History Club.

Harbottle, A.H.H. 1950. 'The occurrence of *Pontia daplidice* Linn. in North Cornwall in 1945'. *Entomologist's Gazette* 1, 49–50.

Harper, G.W. and Waller, W.E. 1950. 'Notes on breeding the first generation of *Polygonia c-album*'. *Entomologist* 83, 145–8.

Harris, P. 2003. 'A Red Admiral Courtship'. *The Butterfly Observer* (24th edn. Winter).

Heath, J., Pollard, E. and Thomas, J.A. 1984. *Atlas of Butterflies in Britain and Ireland.* Penguin Books, Harmonsworth.

Hicks, M.E. and Hale, J.W. 1998. *Lepidoptera of St Agnes, Isles of Scilly. A systematic list and analysis of the species recorded on St Agnes 1992–1997.* Privately published.

Hobson, R., Bourn, N.A.D., Warren, M.S. and Brereton, T.M. 2001. *The Marsh Fritillary in England: A Review of Status and Habitat Condition.* Butterfly Conservation, Wareham.

Hobson, R. and Budd, P. 2001. *The Marsh Fritillary in Cornwall – Site Dossier.* Butterfly Conservation, Wareham.

Hoskin, S.D. 2000. *High Brown Fritillary breeding programme.* Unpublished report for English Nature.

Insect Line, 2002. 'Migrant butterflies during 2001'. *Atropos* 15, 26–30.

Lane, R. 2000a. 'Large Tortoiseshell (*Nymphalis polychloros*), Pontsmill, 4th March 2000'. *The Butterfly Observer* (16th edn. Spring), 5–7.

Lane, R. 2000b. 'Possible American Painted Lady (*Cynthia virginiensis*) at Black Head, Trenarren, near St Austell. *The Butterfly Observer* (18th edn. Winter), 5–6.

Lane, R. 2000c. 'Probable Pale Clouded Yellow, female, Holmbush, 29th Sept. 2002'. *The Butterfly Observer* (18th edn. Winter), 10–13.

Lane, R. 2001. 'Painted Lady – immigrations during the 2000/2001 Winter'. *The Butterfly Observer* (20th edn. Autumn), 12–14.

Lane, R. 2002. 'A White Admiral at Pontsmill'. *The Butterfly Observer* (21st edn. Winter), 4–6.

Lee, M. 2002. *The Occurrence of the Large Blue Butterfly* (Maculinea arion L.) *in Cornwall.* Publication forthcoming.

Maddocks, J. 2002. 'Highlights of the 2001 season'. *Newsletter* 57, 4. Kent Branch, Butterfly Conservation, Fife.

Mendel, H. and Parsons, E. 1987. 'Observations on the life-history of the Silver-studded Blue, *Plebejus argus* L.' *Trans. Suffolk Nat. Soc.* 23, 2–8. Ipswich.

Meneer, R. 1974. *Wildlife Revival in Cornish Hedges.* Dyllansow Truran Publications, Redruth.

Mitchell, A. 1996. *Trees of Britain.* Harper Collins, London.

Morton, A.C.G. 1985. *The population biology of an insect with a restricted distribution*; Cupido minimus *Fuessly.* Unpublished PhD thesis, University of Southampton.

Penhallurick, R.D. 1996. *The Butterflies of Cornwall and the Isles of Scilly.* Dyllansow Pengwella, Truro.

Pullin, A.S. (ed.) 1995. *The ecology and conservation of butterflies.* Chapman and Hall, London.

Ravenscroft, N.O.M. and Warren, M.S. 1996. *Species Action Plan Silver-studded Blue Plebejus argus.* Butterfly Conservation, Wareham.

Roer, H. 1968. 'Weitere Untersuchungen über die Aus-wirkungen der Witterung auf Richtung und Distanz der Fluge des Kleinen Fuchses (*Aglais urticae* L.) im Rheinland'. *Decheniana* 120, 313–334.

Russell, V. 1971. *West Penwith Survey.* Cornwall Archaeological Society, Truro.

Russwurm, A.D.A. 1978. *Aberrations of British Butterflies.* E.W. Classey, Farringdon.

Simpson, M.S.L. 1974. 'Butterflies in the Isles of Scilly, June 1973'. *Bulletin Amateur Entomological Soc.* 33, 91–6.

Smith, F.H.N. 1960. 'A Cornish Note on the 1959 Season'. *Entomologist's Record and Journ. of Variation* 72, 11–12.

Smith, F.H.N. 1997. *The Moths and Butterflies of Cornwall and the Isles of Scilly.* Gem Publishing Co., Wallingford.

Smith, R.T. and Taylor, J.A. (eds) 1995. *Bracken: an environmental issue.* The International Bracken Group, Leeds.

South, R. 1906. *The Butterflies of the British Isles.* Warne, London.

South, R. (ed. Edelsten, H.M. *et al.*) 1941. *The Butterflies of the British Isles.* Warne, London.

Spalding, A. 1990. 'Unusual second brood emergences in Cornwall 1989'. *Entomologist's Record and Journ. of Variation* 102, 84–5.

Spalding, A. 1992. *Cornwall's Butterfly and Moth Heritage.* Twelveheads Press, Truro.

Spalding, A. 1995. 'A review of the status of the Grayling butterfly (*Hipparchia semele* L.; Lepidoptera: Nymphalidae) in Cornwall'. *Biological Recording In Cornwall and the Scillies* 1, 20–4. Cornwall Biological Records Unit, Truro.

Spalding, A. (ed.) 1997. *Red Data Book for Cornwall and the Isles of Scilly.* Croceago Press, Praze-an-Beeble.

Spalding, A. 1998. *The status of the High Brown Fritillary.* (Argynnis adippe) in *Cornwall* 1997. Unpublished report for English Nature. Spalding Associates (Environmental) Ltd., Truro.

Spalding, A. and Haes, E.C.M. 1995. 'Contaminated Land – a Resource for Wildlife: a Review and Survey of Insects on Metalliferous Mine Sites in Cornwall'. *Journ. of Land Contamination and Reclamation* 3, 25–9.

Spalding, A. and Sargeant, P. 2000. *The Wildlife Heritage of the Isles of Scilly.* Twelveheads Press, Truro.

Spalding A. and Tremewan, W.G. 1998. 'Butterflies on St Michael's Mount, Cornwall'. *Entomologist's Gazette* 49, 2.

Spalding, A. with Bourn, N. 2000. *Regional Action Plan: South-West England.* Butterfly Conservation, Dedham.

Thomas, A.C. 1966. 'The character and origins of Roman Dumnonia', In (ed.) Thomas, C. *Rural Settlement in Roman Britain.* Council for British Archaeology, London.

Thomas, A.C. 1985. *Exploration of a Drowned Landscape. Archaeology and History of the Isles of Scilly.* B.T. Batsford Ltd., London.

Thomas, C.D. 1983. *The ecology and status of Plebejus argus L. in north-west Britain.* Unpublished M.Sc. thesis, University College of North Wales, Bangor.

Thomas, J. and Lewington, R. 1991. *The Butterflies of Britain and Ireland.* Dorling Kindersley, London.

Tremewan, W.G. 1956. 'Notes from Cornwall'. *Entomologist's Record and Journ. of Variation* 68, 61–4.

Tucker, J.M. 1991. *The Red Admiral,* Vanessa atalanta. *Problems posed by the hibernation and migration habits of the species.* British Butterfly Conservation. Occasional paper No.1, Colchester.

Tunmore, M. 2000. '1999 Monarch (*Danaus plexippus,* Linn.) influx into the British Isles'. *Atropos* 9, 4–16.

UK Biodiversity Group 1999. *Tranche 2 Action Plan: Invertebrates,* English Nature, Peterborough.

UK Steering Group Report 1995. *Biodiversity: the UK Steering Group Report, Vol.2: Action Plans.* HMSO, London.

Wacher, J.S. 1998a. 'Essex Skipper in West Cornwall'. *The Butterfly Observer* (13th edn. Winter), 10.

Wacher, J.S. 1998b. 'Pale Clouded Yellow at Gwithian Towans', *The Butterfly Observer* (13th edn. Winter), 11.

Wacher, J.S. 1998c. 'Successful overwintering of Painted Lady Cynthia cardui in the U.K.' *Atropos* 5 19–20.

Wacher, J.S. 2002. 'A Second Brood Silver-studded Blue Plebejus argus (Linn.)'. *Atropos* 15, 11–14.

Warren, M.S. 1995. 'Managing local microclimates for the High Brown Fritillary' In (ed.) Pullin, A.S. *The ecology and conservation of butterflies* 198–210. Chapman and Hall, London.

Warren, M.S. and Oates, M.R. 1995. 'The importance of Bracken habitats to fritillary butterflies and their management for conservation,' In (eds) Smith, R.T. and Taylor, J.A., *Bracken: an environmental issue,* 178–81. The International Bracken Group, Leeds.

GAZETTEER

Angarrack	SW 5838	Gear Sands	SW 7655	Looe	SX 2553
Annet (I.o.S)	SV 8608	Godolphin	SW 6031	Lostwithiel	SX 1059
		Godrevy	SW 5842	Luckett	SX 3972
Backways Cove	SX 0485	Goldsithney	SW 5430	Ludgvan	SW5033
Barteliver Wood	SW 9247	Goss Moor	SW 9360	Luxulyan	SX 0558
Binner Downs	SW 6133	Grampound	SW 9348	Lynher Valley	SX 3757
Bochym	SW 6920	Great Arthur (I.o.S.)	SV 9413		
Bodinnick	SX 1352	Great Ganilly (I.o.S.)	SV 9414	Madron	SW 4531
Bodmin	SX 0767	Great Innisvouls (I.o.S.)	SV 9514	Marazion	SW 5130
Bodmin Beacon	SX 1979	Gribben Head	SX 0949	Marsland (and Welcombe)	
Boscastle	SX 0990	Gugh (I.o.S.)	SV 8908	Nature Reserve	SS 2117
Boscundle	SX 0453	Gwendreath	SW 7317		
Botallack	SW 3633	Gwennap Head	SW 3621	Menawethan (I.o.S.)	SV 9513
Breney Common	SX 0561	Gwinear	SW 5937	Mexico Towans	SW 5538
Bryher (I.o.S.)	SV 8715	Gwithian	SW 5841	Millook	SX 1899
Bude	SS 2006			Morwenstow	SS 2015
		Hannafore Point	SX 2552	Mousehole	SW 4626
Calstock	SX 4368	Hartland (Devon)	SS 2624	Mullion	SW 6719
Camborne	SW 6539	Hawks Tor	SX 2576	Mylor	SW 8036
Camel estuary	SW 9277	Hayle	SW 5637		
Camelford	SX 1083	Helford River	SW 7626	Newlyn East	SW 8256
Cancleave	SS 1799	Helston	SW 6628	Newmill	SW 4534
Cape Cornwall	SW 3431	Hensbarrow	SW 9957	New Mills	SX 1191
Carbis Bay	SW 5238	Herodsfoot	SX 2160	North Hill	SX 2776
Carharrack	SW 7341	Higher Crankan	SW 4634		
Carloggas Downs	SX 0156	Hingston Down	SX 3871	Otterham	SX 1690
Carnanton Woods	SW 8863	Holmbush	SX 0452		
Carnmenellis	SW 6936	Holywell Bay	SW 7659	Padstow	SW 9157
Colvannick Marsh	SX 1271			Par	SX 0753
Connor Downs	SW 5939	Kelynack	SW 3730	Park Shady	SW 7047
Coombe Valley	SS 2111	Kenidjack	SW 3532	Penberthy	SW 3255
Constantine	SW 7329	Kennack Sands	SW 7316	Pendeen	SW 3834
Coverack	SW 7818	Keveral Wood	SX 2955	Pendennis	SW 8231
Cremyll	SX 4553	Kilkhampton Common	SS 2511	Penhale Sands	SW 7757
Criggan Moor	SX 0161	King Harry Ferry	SW 8439	Penhallow	SW 8255
Cudden Point	SW 5427	Kynance	SW 6813	Penlee Point	SX 4349
Cusgarne	SW 7540			Pentewan	SX 0147
		Lamorna	SW 4523	Penzance	SW 4730
Daymer Bay	SW 9277	Lamorran Woods	SW 8842	Perran Downs	SW 5530
Deer Park Wood	SX 3973	Land's End	SW 3425	Perranporth	SW 7554
Delabole	SX 0783	Landulph Marsh	SX 4361	Perransands	SW 5329
Dodman Point	SX 0039	Lanhydrock	SX 0863	Perranuthnoe	SW 5329
Downderry	SX 3154	Lansallos Cove	SX 1751	Phillack	SW 5638
Drannock	SW 5836	Lantivet	SX 1650	Polbathic	SX 3456
Dunmere	SX 0468	Launceston	SX 3384	Polperro	SX 2050
		Lelant	SW 5437	Polruan	SX 1250
Ellenglaze Valley	SW 7757	Lewannick	SX 2780	Polscoe	SX 1160
		Liskeard	SX 2564	Polstreath	SX 0145
Falmouth	SW 8132	Lizard	SW 7012	Polyphant	SX 2681
Feock	SW 8238	Loe Bar and Pool	SW 6425	Polzeath	SW 9378
Fowey	SX 1251	Longrock	SW 4931	Pontsmill	SX 0756

Porthcurno	SW 3822	St Just-in-Penwith	SW 3731	Tresco (I.o.S.)	SV 8915
Porthgwarra	SW 3721	St Keverne	SW 9721	Treskilling Downs	SX 0357
Porthleven	SW 6225	St Martin-by-Looe	SX 2654	Treswithian	SW 6241
Porthmeor Cove	SW 4237	St Martin's (I.o.S.)	SV 9216	Trevarno	SW 6430
Portholland	SW 9541	St Mary's (I.o.S.)	SV 9111	Trevissick Farm	SW 7047
Porthtowan	SW 6947	St Mawes	SW 8433	Trevose Head	SW 8576
Portmellon	SX 0143	St Merryn	SW 8874	Trewavas Head	SW 5926
Portreath	SW 6545	St Michael's Mount	SW 5129	Truro	SW 8245
Poundstock	SX 2099	St Michael Penkevil	SW 8542	Truthwall	SW 5232
Priest's Cove	SW 3531	St Minver	SW 9677	Tuckingmill	SX 0977
		Samson (I.o.S.)	SV 8712		
Rame Head	SX 4249	Scorrier	SW 7244	Upton Towans	SW 5740
Red Lake	SX 1258	Seaton Valley	SX 3054		
Red Moor	SX 0762	Sennen	SW 3526	Valency Valley	SX 1291
Rinsey	SW 5927	Sheviock Wood	SX 3755		
Riviere Towans	SW 5538	Sladesbridge	SX 0171	Wadebridge	SW 9072
Rock	SW 9375	Stithians	SW 7336	Welcombe	see *Marsland*
Rosevear (I.o.S.)	SV 8306	Stoke Climsland	SX 3674	Werrington	SX 3287
Rough Tor	SX 1480	Stratton	SS 2306	Western Rocks (I.o.S.)	SV 8306
Ruan Minor	SW 7215			Wheal Alfred	SW 5736
		Talland	SX 2351	Wheal Busy	SW 7344
St Agnes	SW 7150	Tamar Valley	SX 4359	Wheal Carpenter	SW 5835
St Agnes (I.o.S.)	SV 8808	Tean (I.o.S.)	SV 9016	Wheal Cock	SW 3634
St Austell	SX 0152	Tehidy Woods	SW 6443	Wheal Maid	SW 7442
St Breward	SX 0977	Tidna	SS 2014	Wheal Rose	SW 7144
St Cleer Common	SX 2468	Tintagel	SX 0588	White Island (I.o.S.)	SV 8712
St Columb Major	SW 9163	Trebartha	SX 2677	Whitesand Bay	SX 3653
St Erth	SW 5535	Tregantle	SX 3852	Windmill Farm	SW 6915
St Germans	SX 3557	Tregonning Hill	SW 6029		
St Helen's (I.o.S.)	SV 9017	Tregoss Moor	SW 9760	Zelah	SW 8151
St John	SX 4152	Trencrom	SW 5136	Zennor	SW 4538

APPENDIX

Larval foodplants and nectar sources

Larval foodplants

Agrimony (*Agrimonia eupatoria*)
Alder Buckthorn (*Frangula alnus*)
Annual Meadow-grass (*Poa annua*)
Bilberry (*Vaccinium myrtillus*)
Birch (*Betula* spp.)
Bitter-vetch (*Lathyrus linifolius* var. montanus)
Black Bent (*Agrostis gigantea*)
Blackberry (*Rubus fruticosus*)
Black Medick (*Medicago lupulina*)
Blackthorn (*Prunus spinosa*)
Bristle Bent (*Agrostis curtisii*)
Broom (*Cytisus* spp.)
Bullace (*Prunus domestica* ssp. insititia)
Charlock (*Sinapis arvensis*)
Clover (*Trifolium* spp.)
Cock's-foot (*Dactylis glomerata*)
Common Bent (*Agrostis capillaris*)
Common Bird's-foot Trefoil (*Lotus corniculatus*)
Common-couch (*Elytrigia repens*)
Common Cow-wheat (*Melampyrum pratense* ssp. pratense)
Common Stork's-bill (*Erodium cicutarium*)
Creeping Bent (*Agrostis stolonifera*)
Creeping Cinquefoil (*Potentilla reptans*)
Creeping Soft-grass (*Holcus mollis*)
Crown Vetch (*Securigera varia*)
cruciferae
Currant (*Ribes* spp.)
Devil's-bit Scabious (*Succisa pratensis*)
Dock (*Rumex* spp.)
Dogwood (*Cornus sanguinea*)
Dove's-foot Crane's-bill (*Geranium molle*)
Dyer's Greenweed (*Genista tinctoria*)
Early Hair-grass (*Aira praecox*)
Elm (*Ulmus* spp.)
Everlasting Pea (*Lathyrus latifolius*)
False Brome (*Brachypodium sylvaticum*)
Foxglove (*Digitalis purpurea*)
Garlic Mustard (*Alliaria petiolata*)
Germander Speedwell (*Veronica chaemaedrys*)
Globe Artichoke (*Cynara scolymus*)
Gorse (*Ulex* spp.)
Greater Bird's-foot Trefoil (*Lotus pedunculatus*)

Hairy Rockcress (*Arabis hirsuta*)
Heaths (*Erica* spp.)
Hedge Mustard (*Sisymbrium officinale*)
Holly (*Ilex aquifolium*)
Honesty (*Lunaria annua*)
Honeysuckle (*Lonicera periclymenum*)
Hop (*Humulus lupulus*)
Horseradish (*Armoracia rusticana*)
Horseshoe Vetch (*Hippocreppis comosa*)
Ivy (*Hedera helix* ssp. hibernica)
Kidney Vetch (*Anthyllis vulneraria*)
Lady's Smock (*Cardamine pratensis*)
Lesser Celandine (*Ranunculus ficaria*)
Lesser Trefoil (*Trifolium dubium*)
Ling (*Calluna vulgaris*)
Lucerne (*Medicago sativa*)
Mallow (*Malva* spp.)
Marram Grass (*Ammophila arenaria*)
Meadow Vetchling (*Lathyrus pratensis*)
Milkweed (*Asclepias* spp.)
Nasturtium (*Tropaeolum majus*)
Nettle (*Urtica* spp.)
Oak (*Quercus* spp.)
Pansy (*Viola* spp.)
Pellitory-of-the-Wall (*Parietaria judaica*)
Petty Whin (*Genista anglica*)
Poplar (*Populus* spp.)
Purging Buckthorn (*Rhamnus catharticus*)
Purple Moor-grass (*Molinia caerulea*)
Red Fescue (*Festuca rubra*)
Restharrow (*Ononis repens*)
Ribwort Plantain (*Plantago lanceolata*)
Rock-rose (*Helianthemum* spp.)
Seakale (*Crambe maritima*)
Sea Radish (*Raphanas raphanistrum* ssp. maritimus)
Sheep's-fescue (*Festuca ovina*)
Silverweed (*Potentilla anserina*)
Snowberry (*Symphoricarpos* spp.)
Sorrel (*Rumex* spp.)
Spindle (*Euonymus europaeus*)
Thistle (*Cirsium* spp.)
Timothy (*Phleum pratense*)
Torgrass (*Brachypodium pinnatum*)
Tormentil (*Potentilla erecta*)
Tufted Hair-grass (*Deschampsia cespitosa*)

Tufted Vetch (*Vicia cracca*)
Violet (*Viola* spp.)
Viper's-bugloss (*Echium vulgare*)
Virginia Stock (*Malcolmia maritima*)
Wallflower (*Erysimum cheiri*)
Watercress (*Rorippa nasturtium-aquaticum*)
Wavy Hair-grass (*Deschampsia flexuosa*)
Wild Cabbage (*Brassica oloracea* var. oloracea)
Wild Marjoram (*Origanum vulgare*)
Wild Mignonette (*Reseda lutea*)
Wild Strawberry (*Fragaria vesca*)
Wild Thyme (*Thymus polytrichus*)
Willow (*Salix* spp.)
Wood Sage (*Teucrium scorodonia*)
Yarrow (*Achillea millefolium*)
Yorkshire Fog (*Holcus lanatus*)

Nectar sources

Alder Buckthorn (*Frangula alnus*)
Aubretia (*Aubrieta deltoidea*)
Bramble (*Rubus* spp.)
Buddleja (*Buddleja davidii*)
Clover (*Trifolium* spp.)
Common Ragwort (*Senecio jacobaea*)
Cow Parsley (*Anthriscus sylvestris*)
Erigeron spp.
Heath Lobelia (*Lobelia urens*)
Heather spp.
Hemp Agrimony (*Eupatorium cannabinum*)
Ivy (*Hedera* spp.)
Knapweed (*Centaurea* spp.)
London Pride (*Saxifraga umbrosa* × s. spathularis)
Lucerne (*Medicago sativa*)
Michaelmas Daisy (*Aster* spp.)
mud
Privet (*Ligustrum vulgare*)
Red Valerian (*Centranthus ruber*)
rotten fruit
Sedum spp.
Teasel (*Dipsacus* spp.)
thistles

INDEX

Page numbers in **bold** are the main **Species** descriptions which include particulars of the butterflies in Cornwall, habitats and ecology, causes of decline or increase, conservation, larval foodplants, aberrations, flight periods and distribution in the county which are standard entries for almost every species; matters within them are not separately indexed.

A list of larval foodplants and nectar sources is contained in the Appendix (p. 134). **Places** in Cornwall can be found in the **Gazetteer.**